Praise for *Sensory Activ*

MW00579655

Sensory Activities for Autism is an incredible book for teachers and parents. Each sense has it's own list of activities and each activity gives you all of the details you need in a simple, easy to read format. Sensory integration is so important and, as a special education teacher, it's great to see such a comprehensive list of fun learning games for the five senses. Your kids are sure to love them!

— Stephanie DeLussey,
Special Education Teacher and Author of *Mrs. D's Corner*

This is a must have resource for any classroom that specializes in working with children on the Autism Spectrum or any child with sensory needs. It's packed full of fun, hands-on, and engaging learning activities and games that I know my students are going to love. I especially love that the author included activities for all of the five senses and that these are all categorized. This makes it easy to find just the right activity based on my students' sensory needs. I love the simple layout and easy to follow directions, and the majority of the supplies needed are simple household items I already have on hand.

— Traci Bender,
Special Education Teacher, Curriculum Designer, *Blogger at The Bender Bunch*

We all know how beneficial sensory activities are, but finding the time to plan and think of new fun and engaging activities can be tough. Not anymore! This book is filled with amazing activities to work on all of your senses. With quick and easy to follow directions, this book will make planning sensory activities a breeze for you. From explosive lava lamp creations to ooey-gooey spaghetti, this book has it all. A must-have for any education professional, therapist or parent who is looking to make learning fun, and to provide sensory opportunities. This book will be a staple piece of my planning for all sensory learning moving forward. You will not be disappointed.

— Nikki Robertson,
Curriculum Developer and Autism Specialist at *Teaching Autism*

"Forget the kids, try these activities for yourself! Who wouldn't want to discover dinosaurs in ice melts, squish gooey spaghetti, be on cloud nine with fluffy flour dough, slap your smackers around Slippery Jolly Jell-O Balls, then relax to the rhythm of rain! *Sensory Activities for Autism* is a book full of wonder. Do yourself a favour and dive right in."

— *Kathy Hoopman,*
author of *All Cats Have Asperger Syndrome* and *The Spectrum Series*

SENSORY ACTIVITIES FOR AUTISM

Fun Learning Games for Autism and Sensory Disorders

BY MARY MCPHEE

Illustrations by Seth Priske

Edx Autism Publishing www.autismhandbooks.com

Visit the book's website. Comments and new ideas are welcome!
www.autismhandbooks.com

ISBN: 978-0-9951576-6-8
eISBN: 978-0-9951576-7-5

Table of Contents

Introduction

This book is full of tailor-made, easy-to-follow activities to help children — whether they are on the autism spectrum or having difficulties with sensory processing disorder — develop their sensory skills. There are five sets of activities divided into the categories of sight, sound, smell, taste, and touch. Some of the activities work on more than one sensory skill at a time.

Most of the ideas in this book have been contributed by various educators who engage in sensory activities with children on a daily basis. This book is meant to be a valuable resource for your family or for the children you work with.

You'll also notice a few drawings included with the activities in this book. These drawings were created by an artist on the autism spectrum, Seth Priske. He discovered his love for art at an early age and now, he is known for his full-page, felt-tip, brightly-colored art pieces.

How to Use this Book

This book is organized in a choose-your-own-adventure style. You're a busy parent (or teacher), so you don't need to read this book from cover-to-cover (unless you really want to). You can easily glance through the Table of Contents to choose an activity based on the senses of touch, sound, smell, sight, and taste.

Here are some guidelines to follow:

There's no need to read this book from beginning to end. Choose the activities that will be best suited to helping your child develop sensory skills. Every child has their unique strengths and challenges. Look at the adaptation ideas in this book for each activity under the "Added Value" and "Taking it Higher" sections to make any necessary adaptations to match the child's developmental or skill level.

Don't keep this book for yourself. If you know of a parent or teacher that can use some of the sensory activity ideas in this book, share it with them! This activity manual is also great for babysitters or tutors, as it is common to run out of new ideas to keep children engaged.

We're always open to ideas. Do you have an idea for a sensory activity? Send your suggestion to **info@edxautism.com.** We love to hear from parents and teachers.

Keep it fun! Kids learn best when they are having fun. Take note of the child's favorite activities and work those into your regular routine.

Sight

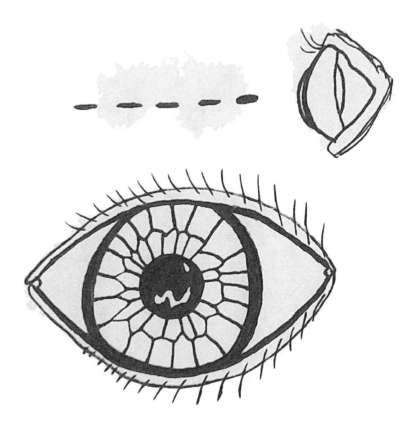

Sensory Slime

Everyone loves cocoa, especially on cold wintery days. Here is an experience using tactile senses, with visuals that are fun to watch, too. Children will complete this hands-on activity to experience how ingredients can change and interact.

Cocoa has a rich chocolate smell to tempt the senses — but keep in mind that this activity is not edible. When the baking soda and vinegar combine, the resulting bubbles and fizz make this creation great for an exciting visual sensory experience. Watch the reaction of the baking soda and the vinegar, and listen for the fizz of the cocoa slime.

What You Need:
- 2 cups corn flour
- ¼ cup baking soda
- 1 envelope cocoa mix
- 1 cup water
- ¼ cup vinegar
- Mixing bowl
- Spoon

Steps:
1. Mix the dry ingredients, corn starch, cocoa powder, and baking soda in a bowl.
2. Add the water slowly and mix well.
3. Now add drops of vinegar to the mix and stir some more.
4. Experience how the mixture reacts.

Added value:

There are several talking points surrounding this experiment. Discuss the sight of the brown cocoa powder blending with the white cornstarch. The sound of the baking soda fizzing with the vinegar. The feel of the slime as it is mixed together. Remember — this is not a taste activity. Pull and stretch the slime and enjoy the cocoa scent as you do so.

Taking it higher:

It could be fun to try other scents instead of cocoa in the mix. Jell-O powder or food coloring could be incorporated to add new color and a different smell to the slime. Leave out one ingredient to find out which one creates the fizz. See if your cocoa slime can run down a baking tray, just like a muddy river. Talk about how slowly the slime moves compared with a mixture of just cocoa and water. Discuss why one is more fluid than the other.

Ice Painting

Looking for an activity to help you cool down? In this activity, kids will use ice to make beautiful paint designs. You can also use this to practice the child's counting, colors, patterns, or whatever else you can think of. For older children, talk about the ice going from a solid state to a liquid state for more of a science lesson!

Note: This can be a messy activity. Make sure to cover the activity space or try this activity outdoors.

What You Need:
- Liquid tempera paint
- Ice cube tray
- Wooden craft sticks or popsicle sticks
- Paper

Steps:
1. Pour different colors of paint into the ice cube tray.
2. Place a popsicle stick into the middle of each cube of paint. (If the popsicle sticks don't stay standing in the middle of the cube, place the tray in the freezer for half an hour before placing the popsicle sticks into each cube. They should be able to stay in the middle at this point.)
3. Place the ice cube tray in the freezer until the paint cubes are frozen.

4. Take a frozen paint popsicle of your choice from the tray and let the child use the ice cube to paint on a white sheet of paper. As the ice melts, the paint leaves a lovely print on the paper. The child can use different frozen ice cubes to make a painting with a variety of colors.

5. Take the opportunity to talk about freezing states, solid states, and liquid states. What happens to the paint when it is in the freezer? What happens as the paint warms and melts onto the paper?

Painting with Cotton Balls

This has to be one of the most entertaining painting activities: it's actually explosive. Paint blobs are laid out strategically on the paper, then round cotton circles are placed carefully over the paint blobs, and then — POW! — the cotton is smashed with a mallet or hammer and the paint sprays out. A creative resist design emerges as the paint is sprayed from around the edges of the cotton circle. Everyone loves the excitement of the splat, and the artistic opportunities are interesting.

You'll also enjoy the added bonus to this activity. The physical action of hammering with a mallet is fantastic for building muscle and those important gross motor skills. Pounding, banging, and aiming for a particular spot help increase eye-hand coordination, too.

What You Need:
- Washable paint
- Round cotton balls
- Paper (long pieces of butcher's paper works well)
- Mallet of rubber hammer
- Apron or old shirt
- Goggles could be a fun extra to keep paint from splatting into eyes

Steps:
1. Prepare paper, paint, and area to be used. This will be messy.
2. Spread out the paper to be splattered on. Use individual sheets or a long spread to make a collage.
3. Put generous blobs on the paper, using a reasonable amount of paint. Then, cover each pile with a round cotton circle.
4. Get geared up for the blob blasting. Put on an old shirt to protect your clothes from flying drops of paint. Wear goggles, if you have some, to protect your eyes from unwanted splats. Then, you're ready to go.

You could dramatize this activity by adding helmets and gloves, like a demolition crew.

5. Smash each cotton circle with one blow of the mallet and watch the paint splat out on all sides.

6. Lift the cotton to reveal your beautiful spatter design.

Taking it higher:

There is an opportunity here for some counting experience, as the blobs can be counted and allocated according to the number of children participating in the big bash. Counting down to the moment the blob is smashed adds both extra fun and backward counting experience, as in "5-4-3-2-1-smash!" Everyone gets a turn, and it is a wonderful social activity with lots of mess and lots of laughter.

Added value:

The collective enjoyment of this activity could lead to the creation of a collage of the splatters — something everyone has participated in. When multiple blobs have been splattered, the effect can be compared to a flower garden. Stalks and leaves added to the blooms will enhance the appearance of a burst of beautiful summer flowers. Adding colorful butterflies and other insects could take the activity further into a nature experience, full of opportunities to explore language and be creative.

Splish Splosh Splatter Painting

Splattering and splashing is a great way to have fun with paint. It is messy, however, so be warned. Splatter paint is best taken outdoors, where creativity can have lots of freedom. Colors will be mixed, and a feeling of sensory abandonment experienced. The initial phase of this activity is controlled indoors, but the joy of splashing paint around is definitely something to appreciate outside.

What You Need:
- White paper
- Painter's tape (masking tape)
- Paint brushes
- Old toothbrushes (optional)
- Mixed paint
- Cups or pots to hold paint
- Plastic apron or old shirt

Steps:
1. Prepare the paper by cutting or tearing off pieces of the painter's tape to mask out a design. This design will resist the paint when it is pulled off after the paint splatters.
2. Prepare the paint. It could be ready-mixed or powder paint you mix to the right consistency. The paint should be quite thick to splatter, not runny.
3. Go outdoors to a place prepared for the splattering. Lay out the paper on a flat surface and then, using one color at a time, show your child how to splish and splosh the paint all over the paper. It is important to

use one color at a time and return the brush to the color it belongs to, so colors do not get mixed up.

4. If you want to add texture to the splatters, use a toothbrush. Dip the bristles into the paint and then tickle the brush with your finger to spray paint onto the paper. Point the paint-filled bristles down and tickle from underneath to avoid spraying your face. Once again, stick to one color for the brush so colors do not get mixed up and murky.

5. Allow the paint to dry before removing the tape. When the tape is removed, the pattern will be revealed where the tape resisted the paint.

Taking it higher:

This is a 'feel good' activity, as paint is allowed to splish and splash everywhere. Take an opportunity to say words like splish, splosh, splat, and splatter as your child splashes the paint around — it's a great way to develop some creative vocabulary. This activity will also encourage organisational skills, because it is important to return the colors to their correct pots. Another teaching point can follow with color matching and learning color names. Parents and teachers can join in the fun and splatter paint, too. Children love to see you get involved.

Added Value:

Using the toothbrush for splattering gives a different texture and adds the unique sensation of tickling the toothbrush. Your child will feel the scratchy tickling of the bristles as they are used to splatter the paint with a finer end result. Try splattering on one side of the paper only, then fold in half to create symmetry or a mirror image of the splats. This can create some very original art.

Then, if you feel like getting really involved with the paint, try a splatter finger paint experience. Hands will be pretty dirty already, so get in and finger paint the splats you've already made for a totally different effect. All these are wonderful sensory experiences.

Look and Listen

Combining a book, picture, or photograph, as an example of the beauty of nature, with a sensory activity is a wonderful way to bring all the senses together under one theme. Find books or magazines that include pictures of natural settings and outdoor experiences, then go on a nature walk and collect some of the real things that you saw in the picture.

Recreating the environment of the animals in the picture also adds to the conversational value of the activity. It's even possible to create a sensory experience that includes the sense of taste. Use the theme of the image to create shaped biscuits that relate back to that idea. The picture stimulates great vocabulary and discussion, and the activity is all about creating a sense of the natural world and the creatures that can be found within it.

What You Need:
- A large tray to be the base of your natural world
- Toys, plastic animals, or pictures of birds or animals you may need to represent the story
- Leaves, grass, dried flowers, twigs — whatever you can find to represent the foliage of a natural world
- Plastic bugs or pictures of creepy-crawlies to hide in your natural world

Steps:
1. Look at the pictures. Discuss the various aspects of nature you can identify.
2. Go into the garden or visit a park to collect the materials for your own natural world.
3. Take time to set up the fantasy nature world by talking about each piece you put in. Feel them, smell them, and listen to the noises they might make in the wind.
4. Talk about the creepy-crawlies and any other creatures they may see in the area.

Taking it higher:

Be sure to feel all the different textures in the natural world. Use the sense of sight to play an "I Spy" game with the things in the natural world. Younger children who are not ready for "I Spy" with letters can use colours, for example: "I spy, with my little eye, something that is red."

Added Value:

The only sense really not applicable to this activity is taste. It would be fun to decorate marshmallows to look like small creatures that might live in the created scene. A plain round marshmallow and some diluted cocoa powder can be used to paint on the features, and use icing to stick on soft sweets to create big eyes. This would be fun to make and then to eat. A grand finale of sensory exploration!

Explosive Lava Lamp Creation

Now, here's an amazing, action-packed activity. Making a lava lamp out of an old water bottle, some cooking oil, and food coloring will give your child an exciting experience. When you drop a fizzy Alka-Seltzer tablet into the mixture, the results will be especially entertaining. Watch the delighted expressions on your child's face and encourage the oohs and aahs of involuntary expression as the tablet does its trick and the colored blobs in the oil move and bubble to the surface.

What You Need:
- An old water bottle
- Cooking oil to fill ⅔ of the bottle
- Food coloring diluted in ½ cup of water
- Alka-Seltzer fizzy tablet

Steps:
1. Fill ⅔ of the empty bottle with oil.
2. Mix the coloring with the ½ cup of water and add to the oil.
3. Break the tablet in half and drop it into the oil.
4. Watch closely to see what happens next!

Taking it higher:

This exercise will get your shy child bursting with excitement at the surprising effect of the fizzy tablet exploding in the oil and water. Organize a countdown scenario before dropping the tablet into the bottle. It is a good way to practice counting backwards. Also, have a discussion about volcanoes, and what lava really is.

Added value:

Line up several bottles in different colors. Add the tablet at different times to see a line of explosions going on simultaneously. Or, try musical explosions. Fill some bottles with less oil and water and then, as they explode, tap the sides to create different 'tunes.' "Three Blind Mice" is an easy song to play with six different-sized bottles and various levels of water. It may take a bit of musical adaptation, but will be fun to try other tunes — and you also have the option of singing along!

Super Simple Sensory Soda Dough

You can't make anything simpler than this sensory dough. The dough has only two main ingredients: water and baking soda. Optional extras can be added to enhance the experience, like introducing color with food coloring or aroma with flavored Kool-Aid powder.

Kool-Aid is an amazing addition to your sensory pantry. It brings out colors and flavors of all sorts of exciting fruits, so take advantage of it to add new sensory experiences to this simple dough recipe.

Try out this simple dough to encourage the sense of touch and smell, along with the added language component of discussing how the dough makes you feel.

What You Need:
- Baking soda
- Water
- Food coloring (optional)
- Kool-Aid powder or essential oils (optional)

Steps:
1. Mix the baking soda with a small quantity of water.
2. Four portions of dough can be using 2 cups of baking soda mixed with ¼ cup of water.
3. Mix the water in slowly until you achieve the right consistency.
4. Add the Kool-Aid as you go and watch for some fizzy reactions.
5. Make different colors for variety and add essential oils with food coloring for a scent and color sensory experience if you prefer not to use Kool-Aid.
6. Store the balls of soda dough in zip-lock bags in the fridge.

Taking it higher:

This activity calls for full involvement, from the start of the preparation through to the finish. Allow your child, if age-appropriate, to take part in the mixing and kneading process. There are great language opportunities at this stage of the process.

Use the addition of Kool-Aid or colorants to your advantage and bring in the senses of sight and smell. Roll the dough into different balls and pretend to smell them as if they were fruits. Kool-Aid has some lovely fruity flavors to use, or essential oils can provide perfumes like lavender and rose. Always be on the lookout for opportunities to develop language, as each color and aroma can be described.

Added value:

This could be an opportunity to play a "guess the scent" game. After discussing all the smells of the different balls of dough, you can try this blindfold game. Blindfold your child and pass around the balls of dough, one at a time, to see who can guess the flavor of each scented ball. Finally, after the game is over, you could roll up the balls and join them together to make a scented caterpillar. Link the balls together, end to end, on a tray and add some pipe cleaner feelers for fun. This could happily lead into fun discussions about caterpillars and butterflies.

Painting with Nature

Mother Nature is an amazing source of creative arts and crafts materials. Imagine making your own paintbrushes from natural materials from your own garden? This activity is a lot of fun for anyone, but may be more suited to slightly older children who are able to go out on a nature walk into the garden and choose different items for their paint brushes before making them and painting with them.

What You Need:
- Sticks
- Elastic bands or string
- Plant and natural materials from the garden
- Scissors or garden cutters (supervise young children carefully)
- Container to collect in the garden — a box or a basket
- Paper and paint

Steps:
1. Prepare to gather natural materials. Show some examples and explain to the children that the object is to find things they can paint with.
2. You can collect the sticks, too, or have them ready and waiting. It is a good idea to have the elastic bands already wrapped around the sticks, to prevent damage to the plants. Just slip the flower stalk under the wrapped elastic band.
3. Bring your gathered materials to assemble the paint brushes.
4. Practice 'painting' with the different brushes you have made.
5. Pattern making would be a great way to show the different textures resulting from using different plants, flowers, feathers, and grasses.

Taking it higher:

There is so much to be gained by going out and looking at nature. It's a social occasion as well as an opportunity to learn about nature, like the parts of a plant and the differences between flowers, leaves, and stems. You can also talk about how to pick the plants carefully and where to look for other items, like feathers, that may also work for natural brushes.

Added value:

The natural paint brushes would lend themselves well to the creation of leaf or flower prints. A combination of paint techniques can be used as the flower is printed and then painted over with the natural brush. Folding the art paper in half and laying the plant paintbrush on one side, then pressing the other half of the paper over and gently rubbing over the plant creates a mirror image when the paper is opened back up. This is a good opportunity to discuss symmetry with older children.

Color Mixing and Storytime, Too

When storytime and activities can come together, there is a wonderful combination of sensory experiences. Delightful stories can conjure up creative painting ideas. Stories about rainbows,  sunsets, painting, and color blending all lend themselves to pairing learning about color with fantasy and fun. Using a story alongside experimentation with paint helps children learn all about how we get so many different colors. This sensory activity will see kids tune into their sense of hearing to listen to the story, and their sense of seeing as they watch the colors mix together.

What You Need:

- Storybooks or rhymes about color, rainbows, or other beautiful, colorful topics
- Paint colors of your choice, but primary colors of red, blue, and yellow are essential
- Paint pots or containers, along with a palette or ice tray to mix the colors
- Brushes, pipette, sponges, and paper to try out new colors
- Water jar to wash brushes

Steps:

1. Prepare the painting activity first, so the story leads straight into the painting experience. That means the paint colors should be set out with the mixing trays, brushes, and sponges and paper to experiment on.
2. Create an air of anticipation through the "I wonder what we are going to do today?" comments.
3. Read the story and stimulate creative painting ideas or themes.

4. Tell your child that now it is time to paint using the story ideas, enjoying all the colors laid out on the table.

5. Experiment with the pipette by dropping blobs of paint into the paint trays, or dip the sponge tip into the paint and smear it onto the paper to see the lovely color-mixing results.

6. Allow some free-range discovery attempts before showing how the primaries of red, blue, and yellow make secondary colors. The detail of this part depends on age and maturity. If your child just wants to squish and spread paint randomly, that is a great experience, or perhaps your child is ready for a more formal approach. Either way, this sensory activity will be a fun opportunity to give them a great sense of color.

Taking it higher:

Using the sponges extends the experience to include a tactile play session. It would be fun to cut the sponge into an oval, like the shape of a mouse's body. Then, dip the sponge into the different colors. The sponge, with its color or multiple colors, can be dabbed or spread over the paper. Double color effects can be seen when one side of the sponge is dipped in one color and the other side is dipped in another — then, as the sponge is pulled across the page, the two colors will blend together.

Added value:

Fingers and thumbs will get pretty messy during this activity, but that just gives you the opportunity to carry the color idea and the story theme a step further. Make printed thumb prints in the various colors and turn them into little pictures or characters. Thumb prints joined together in a row make wonderful wiggly worms. The sponges filled with different colors can create lovely rainbows as they are dragged in an arch shape across the page. There is so much fun to be had with color — especially when you combine it with a story.

Twinkle Twinkle Finger Paint

This is a gooey — but not too messy — finger paint, with the added sparkle of glitter. This twinkle finger paint has an added visual attraction as it is smoothed and smeared over paper or on a plate, if you prefer. Adding some aroma with Kool Aid provides an extra sensory touch.

The glittery finger paint will feel squishy and look shiny — and, with some Kool Aid, it could be scented with your child's favorite fruity smell.

What You Need:
- 2 cups cold water
- ½ cup corn starch (cornflour)
- 3 tsp sugar
- Liquid watercolor paint or food coloring
- Kool-Aid for aroma (optional)

Steps:
1. Combine the ingredients without the color or aroma to make the basic paint.
2. Put the mixture in a pot on medium heat on the stove.
3. Stir with a whisk until the mixture thickens.
4. This is the basic finger paint — separate into containers to make different colors if you wish to add variety.
5. WARNING: The paint will be hot, so don't use it before you are sure it has cooled down completely.
6. If it becomes lumpy, add some more water and keep mixing.
7. Spread it out on large sheets of paper so everyone can enjoy the sensation of finger painting, and smooth and smear it all over the paper.
8. Or, spread and smooth the paint on a tray or large plate instead of using paper.

Taking it higher:

Kids just love finger paint. It is a great way to encourage some sensory touch and feel experiences. Encourage language development by asking questions about how the paint feels. What is it like as you smooth the paint on the paper? How do you make pictures with the paint? Think of some fun rhyming words to talk about the paint, like "ooey gooey," or "squishy squashy," and "smooth in a groove," and so on — just have fun with these kinds of words.

Added value:

Make some hand-printed fan-tailed pigeons to show off the finger paint. Draw an oval shape for the bird's body, then add a beak with yellow paint and two legs with brown paint. Then, press your hand into the finger paint and press that painted hand onto the paper to make the fan tail of the bird. The tail can be printed several times for added effect. Cut out the birds and hang them up as art — make several for a frieze along the wall.

Rainbow Freeze

For a really unusual way to make building blocks, try freezing colored water in ice trays. Prepare the colored water and then freeze the blocks in the ice trays. When they're ready, press out the frozen cubes and store them in zip-lock bags for use whenever you are in the mood to build.

What You Need:
- Water to fill the ice trays
- Ice trays
- Food color or liquid color paint

Steps:
1. Mix your water and coloring together.
2. Freeze the paint to make the colored blocks.
3. Freeze one color at a time.
4. Empty each color into a separate zip-lock bag and store in the fridge until ready for use.
5. Have bowls ready to holding the cubes once they are frozen.

Taking it higher:

This could be an opportunity for some imaginative fun. Tell your child that Inuit people build houses out of frozen blocks and today, the Inuit are going to get a colorful frozen house. Practice building with the blocks as a builder would to make a strong wall. This means setting the blocks in neat rows, with the second row of blocks set out like a proper wall. Explain why this adds strength to the wall. Sensory experiences of feeling ice-cold blocks while building with them are a valued part of the experience. Added to that, as the blocks melt, children can see solid changing to liquid — and watch colors blend in the melting process.

Added value:

Here is a great opportunity for some ice painting. If you have colored the ice blocks with liquid paint or food coloring, then the blocks of ice can be slid over paper to make a painting in a creative way. Instead of ice skating, tell your child it's time for ice painting. Take the ice and do some skater's moves like circles, loops, and a figure eight.

Magic Milk Glow

Milk is the perfect liquid to use for this magical experiment. The molecules and the fat content in milk react to the introduction of color and dish soap. Watch the colors disappear and return like magic.

What You Need:
- Milk
- Fluorescent paint or watercolors
- Squeezie bottles or pipette
- Dish soap
- Q-tip, toothpick, or craft stick
- Black light

Steps:
1. Fill a shallow pan with enough milk to cover the bottom.
2. Fill the squeezie bottles with watered-down paint. It should be the consistency of food coloring.
3. Squirt little blobs of the colored paint around the edge of the pan with the milk.
4. Dab a q-tip (cotton bud) or other stick mentioned into the dish soap and touch the centre of the milk pan with the tip.
5. Watch the color disappear and then slowly return — like magic.
   (The science behind this activity is that the contents of the milk react to the detergent.)

Taking it higher:

This is a visual sensory experience, and your child will love watching the colors magically swirl and disappear. Then, the colors return, and the fantastical experiment is complete. Let your child describe the experience with words like "amazing," "magical," and "wonderful." Try out different color combinations and see where the experiment takes you.

Added value:

Try to recreate the color patterns on paper. Experiment with other ideas to achieve different effects. Blow bubbles into the milk with a straw and see what foamy colored milk looks like. Instead of paint, use food coloring — then, afterwards, you can put straws into the magic milk and enjoy some magic milkshakes.

I Spy with My Little Eye

The sense of sight is often taken for granted, but this activity shows children how to use this sense with a purpose. Making some play binoculars and experiencing wearing a pirate patch actively engages children in seeing. Looking at small items through a magnifying glass increases their awareness of the objects as they become magnified. The play activities are creative, but the reason behind them is to build on sight sensory skills and to enhance awareness of the things each child can see around them.

What You Need:
- Homemade binoculars using two cardboard tubes
- String
- Cardboard to make an eye patch
- Thin elastic
- Magnifying glass

Steps:
1. Glue the two tubes of cardboard together to make a pair of binoculars. The inner tubes of toilet rolls are perfect for this job. Decorate the binos with paper or stickers or paint. Make two holes at the side for threading the string and measure the string so it will fit over your child's head. There — you have a set of imaginary binoculars!
2. Draw the shape of a pirate's eye patch on a black card, or any color if you want to paint it black. Make holes in the patch and use elastic to thread through two holes on either side of the patch. Tie the elastic to fit your child's head, making sure the patch sits right over their eye.

3. Show your child how a magnifying glass can make things look bigger and more detailed. Select several smaller items from around the house to look at and discuss the differences using a magnifying glass.

Added Value:

Sight isn't just about the act of looking. Encourage your child to develop their sense of sight by observing details. Each of the objects used in this exercise are geared toward gaining a better awareness of the sense of sight.

Taking it Higher:

Kim's game is a wonderful observation game that encourages the use of the sense of sight to capture detail and improve memory skills, too. Place several objects on a tray and allow your child to look at them for a short while (the number of objects and the amount of time will depend on the age of the children). After a minute or two, a cloth is put over the tray and the observer has to recall the items on the tray. This can be done verbally, pictorially, or orally.

Listen and Do with Building Blocks

Here's an interesting activity that involves the senses of sight and sound together, with an added bonus — the use of memory skills. When children are encouraged to use multiple sensory skills, it helps with early development and with practicing essential skills or tools used in learning. The focus of this activity is listening to an explanation of how to complete a task, and then seeing if that task was completed correctly.

What You Need:
- Different sizes and colors of building blocks
- A book or file to put up as a shield between the two children

Steps:
1. Set up two children or an adult and a child at a table opposite each other.
2. Give each person the same number and colors and shapes of building blocks.
3. Set up a barrier or screen between the two.
4. One child creates a pattern with their building blocks, then describes it to the other person.
5. When the second person has heard the description, they copy it with their own blocks.
6. The screen is lifted when the pattern is complete, and then the patterns are checked to see if they match.
7. The roles are reversed and play continues.

Added Value:

This activity is all about combining the sense of hearing with the sense of seeing. Choose different items to create more intricate patterns, like beads or wooden shapes. Hand out papers and pencils for a drawing exercise, with directions of what to draw in the picture. For example, draw a house with a red door and two blue windows. Add other items according to the age and interests of the children.

Taking it Higher:

An activity that allows children to follow directions will boost their sense of hearing. After following directions, there is the satisfaction of seeing the finished work. This concept can be taken higher by using the building blocks to construct something, an actual item. Older children may enjoy origami, paper folding, and following the instructions to make something else out of paper. Paper folding will add in a sense of direction and sizes, too.

Touch

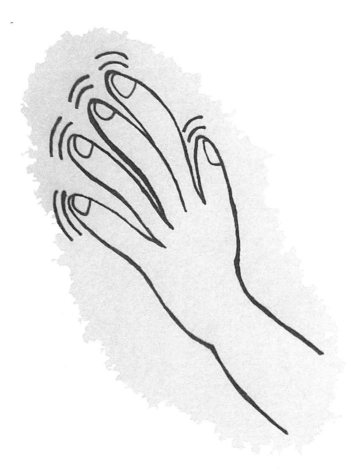

Sensory Table

A sensory table will help children explore and experience their different senses while having fun. They'll be able to sift, sort, dig, or pour. You can make your own version of a sensory table for the home or classroom with this activity.

What You Need:
- Table
- Large and shallow plastic bin or tub
- Large bath towel
- Small dustbin and brush

   Optional:

- **Water** - add soap, food coloring, toys that sink or float, plastic fish, or nets
- **Food** - soft noodles, Jell-O, cornmeal
- **Grains** - rice, cereal, oatmeal, seeds
- **Outdoor** - leaves, grass, twigs, magnifying glasses
- **Items from around the house** - buttons, cotton balls, shaving cream

Steps:
1. Place a large, shallow plastic bin or tub on top of a table. If you don't have a table to place it on, you can place the bin on the floor or outdoors in the yard.
2. Add a large bath towel under the bin to catch any spills that may happen (this is especially important if you're adding water to the bin).
3. Place a small dustbin and brush on the side of the bin and encourage the child to clean up independently if any spills happen.
4. Add your choice of objects from the optional list of suggestions.
5. You can also add your own items such as plastic spoons, empty food containers, etc.

6. Give the child the chance to try independent play and exploration first, and then you can join in and guide the child through play or learning based on the child's learning goals or developmental level. For example, you may want to help the child sort different colored items, or help them observe which items sink or float. Talk or discuss the child's observations, make lists, or just let the children play and have fun trying different things in the sensory bucket.

Added value:

The sensory table is really a great asset for developing the senses. It can be used to either focus on one particular sense at a time, or muddle all the senses together into one sensory overload! Think about each individual sense and you could set them out on different trays or set up sections on your main table. Lay them out one at a time, then mix up some different sensory items for a variety and a "guess the sense I am using" game.

- Smell different items in little jars with lids to contain the scent, using things like lavender, rose petals, spices from the kitchen, toothpaste, soap, and so on.
- Taste different sweet or savory flavors with items on a saucer. It is fun to blindfold your child and see the reaction to lemon, for example, or sherbet with a fizzy surprise element.
- Touch offers another blindfold opportunity, to ensure only the correct sense is in use. Feel things like wool, sandpaper, silk, sponges, and other objects with interesting textures.
- Seeing things under a microscope lends a whole new dimension to your sensory table. If you can, borrow a microscope from a science department, or perhaps just get very strong magnifying glasses to extend your sense of sight.
- Bring out all sorts of things that make sounds. Whistles, bells, squeaky toys, kitchen utensils, voices, and various recordings can all contribute to your sensory sound section of the table. Once again, pop on a blindfold and then play the sound so that, without seeing what made the noise, your child can sense the sound and tell you what it is.

Taking it Higher:

Kim's Game is a wonderful memory game and is good for concentration, recall, and using sensory skills. All you need is a tray and a cloth to cover it. Choose some of the items from the sensory table and set them on the tray. Let your child look at the items for a minute, then cover the items with the cloth and ask your child to use their sense of sight to recall the items on the tray. Another way to recall the items is to draw pictures on a piece of paper to see how many were remembered. Another extension of the idea would be to set items on the tray for the different senses. Use the time to smell, touch, or taste each item, and then cover the tray for your child to recall the items in the different sensory categories using those particular senses. Putting on a blindfold enhances the use of the single sense without the additional use of the sense of sight.

Shredded Paper Art

Some kids on the spectrum love shredding paper. This is your chance to join in the fun and make some art! You can even turn these art pieces into greeting cards for family and friends.

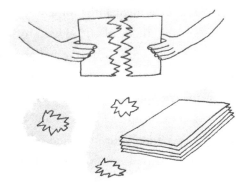

What You Need:

- A white sheet of 11" by 17" paper
- Colored construction paper
- Pencil
- Scissors
- Glue stick

Steps:

1. Have the child pick an idea for an art piece to make with shredded paper — for example, a picture of a bouquet of flowers or a house.

2. If the child needs a visual guide, help them draw an image on a white sheet of paper, where he or she will glue their shredded construction paper to make the art image.

3. Have the child shred sheets of colored construction paper with their hands, which will make up the art piece image. You can also use scissors to cut out construction paper shapes if you want to help the child work on their scissor-cutting skills.

4. Have the child arrange the shredded paper pieces and glue them onto the white sheet of paper to form the desired art piece image. Encourage overlapping of construction paper pieces to make layers and help the art stand out.

Added value:

Paper has wonderful qualities for sensory stimulation — it can scrunch and fold like a fan, and crinkle or curl. Listen to the sounds of scrunching and tearing, and feel the different textures created by folding. Try out different activities with the newspaper by just scrunching a big piece and hearing the sound, as well as feeling the crumpled-up sensation. Then, fold the paper like a fan. Open the fan and look at the texture of the lines and the folds made by this action. Cut a long strip of paper from your piece and roll it around a pencil. Take out the pencil, and the rolled-up piece of paper is left like a curl, giving a different texture and addition to the paper craft.

Taking it Higher:

Use this opportunity to tear the paper into smaller pieces, like squares, and fit them together to design a mosaic. Different colors of paper will add interest to the mosaic. Look at tiles in the kitchen or bathroom and see how the squares fit together to make a tiled pattern. Tissue paper of different colors add texture to the mosaic and can overlap very successfully. Another creative idea is to cut slits along the paper's folded edge, or cut out triangles and then open your folded paper. It will look like a beautiful fan or paper doily. Wave your fan in front of your face and feel the moving air it generates.

Super Sensory Tickle Tub

Touching and feeling is the essence of sensory play. It's important to create opportunities for your child to feel different things — and what better way to do so than to get their hands right into a tub of interesting textures? This will heighten their sense of touch. While sensory defensive children may shy away from feeling different textures, the sensory 'tickle tub' gives them a chance to explore touching different items at their own pace. The experience is all about feeling and expressing the sensations felt at the time.

Choose from an array of edible textures for the very young child who you know will want to experience the sensation of the objects in his mouth. Your pantry will be a good starting point. Cheerios, biscuit crumbs, and sugar lumps are great edible sensory options. Older children enjoy sensory play, too, and will be able to handle wood shavings, colored pasta, collections of buttons, and other plastic items. Only use these when you will be sure the child will not put them in their mouth.

Your tub could also include wet and sticky sensory items, like Jell-O or water beads, ice cubes, and whipped shaving cream. The choice is yours. Think about putting the different dry items into resealable bags, either ready for use at another time or for a textured craft activity.

What You Need:
- Dry sensory items to fill the tickle tub
- Bags or containers to store the items if you choose to reuse them
- A large plastic tub or basin with deep sides
- Plastic cloth or table covering for messy sensory items
- Wet sensory items, if the messy play is chosen

Steps:
1. Putting the tickle tub or sensory bin together initially is simply a matter of organization and making use of items you likely have in your

kitchen. Choose edible items for the toddlers who may still want to explore with their mouths.

2. Put out the items you want to use and make sure there is enough in the tickle tub to make it worthwhile.

3. Set the activity in a convenient play place, and be sure to use a cloth or table covering to ensure any resulting mess is contained.

4. Join in with encouraging words to add language enrichment to the activity.

5. Pack away for future use if the items are in the right condition to be used again.

Added Value:

The tickle tub gives you an opportunity to encourage kids to feel items in different ways — crunching them, spreading them, piling them up, dropping them, and feeling them slip through fingertips. All these sensory actions can be accompanied with language development and social interaction.

Taking it Higher:

Play a game of "hide and seek" by hiding different objects in the sensory materials. Children must put their hands into the sensory area of the tickle tub and search for the hidden items. These could be plastic animals, shapes, or plastic letters of the alphabet. Each item must be felt and described before it can be removed from the basin. An added interest for older children could be to tell them what they must find hidden in the "Tickle Tub."

The Super Sensory Tickle Tub is bound to be a lot of fun for children of many different ages. Talk about tickling before you use the tub for the first time and spread some laughter round the room with an impromptu tickle session!

Mud, Mud, Glorious Mud!

Mud is fascinating for children. It is a gooey, slimy, wet, and sticky all-in-one glorious mess. Allowing children to play with mud and get messy as they create mud pies will always be a favorite. Commercially-made 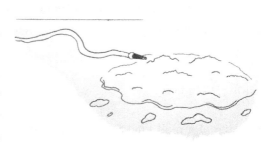 mud kitchens are available, but even without investing in this item, it is still possible to create a mud kitchen of your own.

Your mud kitchen is going to enable messy, muddy play in your own backyard or covered patio — anywhere but in your own kitchen!

What You Need:
- An old tray or tabletop to work on (a sand tray is a good mud kitchen substitute)
- Pots, old plastic cups and plates, utensils — as much as you can supply from the kitchen to keep the mud kitcheners busy
- Different-sized spoons, forks, jugs, and a sieve will be handy, too

Steps:
1. Set up the basis for the kitchen using the best materials you have available to make a safe mud play area.
2. Distribute the mud and sand into containers, ready to mix. Provide useful containers to store the mud items.
3. Make a display of different utensils or set them out in plastic bowls, ready to use.
4. Supply aprons, as this could get messy.
5. Have a bucket of water on-hand to wash up.

Added Value:

Use the mud to create a name plaque. First, set the mud in a tray or in the lid of a box. Before it can set, write your child's name in the mud. When the mud dries, you will have your child's name moulded into the hardened mud produced at the mud kitchen. Have fun creating and moulding specific kinds of food, like donuts and pizza. You can even decorate with plants and flowers from the garden.

Taking it Higher:

Working in a mud kitchen is going to offer loads of language opportunities. Describing the mud as it squishes through your fingers and patting mud cakes together are very tactile sensory opportunities. Use the mud to explore words like "ooze," "squash," "pat," and "roll" — all sensory activities the mud will allow.

Creamy Sand

This is an irresistible slippery, slithery experience with a touch of "true grit." Mixing shaving cream with play sand creates an amazing textured, creamy substance. Children love to feel this unusual sand ooze through their fingers.

It's a good idea to present the creamy sand in a plastic container, so your child can enjoy handling it and smoothing it all around the container. The mixture is smooth and creamy, but at the same time has the hint of texture from the sand.

What You Need:
- Shaving cream
- Play sand
- Large bowl or plastic container
- Whisk or spoon

Steps:
1. Mix the shaving cream and play sand together.
2. Adjust the quantities of sand to cream to make a foamy texture with some elements of sand.
3. Place the mixture into a bowl for everyone to use.

Added Value:

The shaving cream is a real winner for bringing texture to little fingers. Avoid contact with eyes and mouths, however, because shaving cream is soap. This is a great way to introduce two textures in one go — the gritty feeling of the sand and the smooth feeling of the foam.

Taking it Higher:

It would be great fun to lay out some of the foamy cream on a baking tray. Smooth it out and then try different finger activities. Write names or draw patterns and pictures. Cut a serrated edge out of card and scrape that across one of the foamy baking trays to create lovely patterns. An old comb or a fork will make some interesting patterns, too.

Creepy Crawly Sensory Bin

Insects are always a great way to study different senses and different visual impacts. There are so many kinds of insects. Some that creep, some that crawl, and some that wriggle or fly. Putting plastic insects into a sensory bin to touch and feel or find in a different environment can be fun for everyone. Using coffee grounds as dirt makes this an even more fulfilling sensory experience. The touch of the granules and the aroma of coffee together with the feel of the creepy crawlies adds excitement to the activity.

What You Need:
- Used coffee grounds
- Bin or open box
- Plastic insects

Steps:
1. Collect some used coffee grounds at home or from your local coffee shop.
2. Dry them out and spread them at the bottom of a container or box.
3. Hide the plastic insects in the coffee grounds in the box.
4. Dig around and find different insects.

Taking it Higher:

This is a great activity for feeling and describing the insect hidden amongst the coffee grounds. One person feels and finds the insect, and the others guess what it is based on the description. The procedure can be reversed where one person describes the insect they want and the other feels around in the box to locate the desired creepy crawly.

Added Value:

Once you've found an insect in the box of coffee grounds, draw the insect on paper and then outline the drawing in clear glue. Sprinkle the coffee grounds onto the glued outline and dust them over the paper. The coffee grounds will stick to the glue and leave a coffee version of the insect. Allow the design to dry, and then have finger fun by exchanging pictures and, with eyes closed, feeling the design and guessing what insect it is. All these activities encourage the senses of touch and smell, and the visualization of the insects from the creepy crawly sensory bin.

Frozen Iceberg Beads

Frozen water beads look like the pieces of an iceberg as they glisten in the sun. Letting children feel the cold, slippery beads as they slide through their fingers is a great sensory experience. The frozen beads will feel cold at first, but as they thaw, they will not be so icy. This is an interesting sensory contrast to expose the children to. Giving them the opportunity to watch the beads grow in the water prior to being frozen is another fascinating sensory experience. Your child will enjoy feeling the water beads in his hand as they come out of the packet like little colored seeds. Then, add them to the water and watch them grow into full-sized water beads. This is the perfect time for some language development as you talk about growing and increasing in size.

What You Need:
- Water beads like the variety used by florists
- A bowl to soak the beads and watch them grow
- A tray to put them into the freezer and make the frozen beads

Steps:
1. Soak the beads in water until they swell into their proper bead size.
2. Put the beads into a container, then put the container into your freezer.
3. Transfer the frozen beads into a packet and scoop them out to use as needed.
4. Return used beads to the freezer.
5. Put the beads somewhere to let your child handle them and feel the cold sensation of the beads in his hand.
6. Do not try this activity with children who may put these beads in their mouths.

Added Value:

Color sorting and controlling slippery beads could be fun to try. Bring out the ice trays and separate the frozen beads into different colors as a sorting exercise.

You can make the sorting more challenging by giving the sorters some tweezers or sugar cube tongs to lift the frozen beads out of the bowl and into their sorting trays. This is an opportunity to practice fine motor control and sorting at the same time.

Taking it Higher:

Try making frozen bead shapes by gathering some cookie cutters like hearts and stars. Fill the cookie cutter with the water beads and then set them on a tray in the freezer. See what beautiful frozen shapes can be made, and then float them in water. Watch together as they dissolve and the shape disappears.

Super Goo-bleck: Liquid-Solid Slime

Here's a really simple goo that will entertain and educate at the same time. Goo-bleck, or oobleck, was named by Dr Seuss in his book *Bartholomew and the Ooblek*. It is a gooey, slimy solution that will fascinate both young and older children.

Oobleck has scientific name, "non-Newtonian fluid," and it can be felt as a solid or a liquid, depending on how you handle the substance. Dip your hand into a basin of goo-bleck and it will slip through your fingers. Squash and push the goo, and it becomes solid. Two for the price of one, this activity is great fun to both make and play with.

Goo-bleck or oobleck needs very simple ingredients, but can be a bit messy. It is advisable to spread out some newspaper to cover your working surface.

What You Need:
- 1 – 2 cups corn starch
- 1 cup water
- Food coloring (optional)
- A deep mixing bowl
- Willing and able fingers

Steps:
- Measure a cup of cornstarch and gently tip it into a deep bowl.
- Measure the first cup of water and slowly pour it into the bowl, mixing gently with your fingers.
- Keep adding water until the goo reaches the right consistency. You can judge this yourself. More water will make more fluid goo, less water and it will be more solid.

- Add coloring to the water if you want to color the goo.

Now, you are ready to play with the goo-bleck. It can slide through your fingers or you can squash it up into something solid. Let go, and it slips back to a liquid.

Added Value:

Children are fascinated by the goo that can change like magic. This activity encourages wonder and amazement, with an added element of excitement as the children slip their fingers through the slippery goo. Great language and conversation opportunities go hand in hand with this activity. Children who have been to the sea can be reminded of the sinking sand on the beach as the tide comes in.

Taking it Higher:

Super goo-bleck acts just like sinking sand. Make an extra-large quantity and pour it into a big basin, big enough to stand in. Let the children stand in the goo and feel it between their toes. Take slow steps and big, stomping steps to see what happens to the goo as they put more pressure into the water. Older children could talk about solids and liquids and their differences.

Play a game of "swamp monster":

Pretend the goo is a crocodile-infested swamp. The game is to try and get figurines, like army men, across the swamp without being caught by a crocodile.

Line several men on the side of the "swamp" and set a timer. See how many figures each child can get across successfully without having them sink in the goo. They will have to move them carefully, as while they slide over the goo, other figures may be sinking. Lay a plastic crocodile in the middle for fun.

Younger children will enjoy Dr Seuss' story *Bartholomew and the Oobleck*.

Pipe Cleaners, Straws, and Playdough Fun!

Playdough, straws, and pipe cleaners are useful craft materials to have at home. Together, these three items can lend themselves to inspiring building opportunities. Playdough creates a solid base while the pipe cleaners and straws add height and interest to the project. Your child will enjoy experimenting with these items, and this activity suits a variety of ages. Little ones will have fun just sticking the straws and pipe cleaners into the dough, and older children may find the straws and the pipe cleaners can be linked together to make more advanced designs. Encourage creativity and expression of ideas along the way.

What You Need:
- Playdough
- Straws
- Pipe cleaners
- Other creative add-ons, like googly eyes, candles, toothpicks (for older children, due to sharp points) buttons and much more — use your imagination!

Steps:
1. Pre-make the playdough. Quantity will depend on the number of children.
2. Collect straws, cut them into different sizes to add height and interest.
3. Add in the pipe cleaners.
4. Finally, collect other items of interest.
5. Find different containers for the items so they are easy to use for the activity and pack away for another day.

Taking it Higher:

Building and creating using different types of creative materials is a wonderful sensory experience. Children can feel the rough and smooth textures, or compare the lengths of the straws and talk about the different objects they are using.

The playdough acts as a base for a building-type structure when it is flattened, but in a round blob, it could become a creature of some sort. Each item can be discussed in a way that tells everyone what is being made and what it is made out of. Talking about something you have made opens an opportunity for natural conversation between children and adults.

Added Value:

It would be great fun to have a group activity and build a playdough city. Everyone could use their dough to create a house and use chalk to draw some roads for toy cars to drive around the town. Pack-up time with this activity is a chance to practice sorting and getting everything put back into its proper container.

Mess-free busy bee!

Here's a delightful mess-free activity for little ones. An easy-to-make buzzing bee, constructed out of plastic and tape and some pretty charms. This bee, or any other flying bug, is a perfect playmate. Little ones can help in creating the bee or bug and enjoy playing with it once it is complete.

What You Need:
- Extra thick and strong freezer zip-lock bags in a one-gallon capacity size
- A stencil in the shape of wings
- Scissors
- Permanent marker
- Duct tape
- Hair gel
- Sequins and charms
- Pipe cleaners

Steps:
1. Lay two zip-lock plastic bags on top of each other.
2. Put the centre line of the bee or bug shape on the fold of the bags and trace the outline of a bee or bug shaped stencil.
3. Cut out the bee shape but do not cut across the fold mid-line.
4. Open the bee shape so there are two sides to the bee, making the symmetrical shape of the wings.
5. Lay these pieces down opposite each other to form the wings.
6. Seal the edges with duct tape to create a sealed border. Leave a small opening.
7. Fill the opening with sequins or charms.

8. Follow the sequins with the hair gel.
9. Wipe the area and then seal.
10. Place the wings side by side, about an inch apart. Add a strip of tape to join the two and make a bee. The bee or bug looks especially beautiful against the window.

Taking it Higher:

Talking about the parts of the bee or bug as you examine the one you have made is an example of the way the children can be inspired by nature, and the animals that have adapted to their surroundings. Look at symmetry and the patterns on some pictures of insects. Set the bee or bug your child has made into a special place, like the bedroom or kitchen window, where everyone can admire the work of art. Allow the children to play with their new toys.

Added Value:

This is an opportunity to delve into outside museums and books to find other creepy crawlies. Butterflies are magnificent examples of symmetry in nature. Look at their colorful wings and use your imagination to pretend they are ball gowns. Pretend it is time for a butterfly ball, and discuss what it might be like for a butterfly going to a ball. Choose different colors of tissue paper and design another butterfly, but use tissue paper to make the delicate wings. Older children will enjoy looking at the symmetry they can see in bugs, bees, and butterflies, and their delicate wings.

Ice-age Exploration

"Imagine being an explorer in the frozen wastes of the Arctic," you can tell your child, in preparation for the activity today. Arm yourselves with goggles to look super cool and some water to melt the ice letters or plastic animals that are going to be retrieved. This will offer great sensory experiences of hot and cold, as well as liquid and solid, and provides a measure of fantasy play along with help with memorizing simple words.

What You Need:
- Cups or small containers
- Goggles
- Jugs or spray bottles
- Warm water
- Plastic letters or animals
- Tray to hold the ice artifacts

Steps:
1. Prepare your ice exploration cups.
2. Put plastic animals or plastic letters of the alphabet in the cups and fill with water.
3. Freeze the contents of the cups.
4. Take the frozen ice cups and tip them into the tray, ready for exploration.
5. Put on goggles to prevent ice chips flying up into sensitive eyes.
6. Chip away at the ice cups or squirt with water to melt the ice and reveal the animal or hidden letters.
7. Discuss your findings.

Taking it Higher:

Use this as an opportunity to discuss how the ice trapped the animals or the letters. Talk about the temperature of the ice and the water. Experience the excitement of exposing the letters or the animal that was trapped in the ice.

Added Value:

Make a "frozen" picture. Use cellophane paper to represent the ice, then glue different animals under the ice and top off the picture with a layer of cotton wool to represent snow. Find out more about animals that were frozen during the Ice age and have fun watching the animated movie called... *Ice Age*!

Ooey Gooey Spaghetti

This is an irresistible activity for any child who loves getting into slimy stuff. Ooey Gooey Spaghetti ticks all the  boxes for a thrilling touchy-feely experience. Set your spaghetti out in different containers, but be prepared for it to become one great big bowl of slimy noodles.

What You Need:
- Dried spaghetti
- Pot and water to boil
- Cold water
- Food coloring
- Vegetable oil
- Different containers
- Tongs and other utensils to play with

Steps:
1. Cook the spaghetti and cool it down quickly until it is ready to add coloring.
2. Divide the spaghetti into different containers, depending on how many colors you want to use.
3. Add coloring to the spaghetti in the container, along with a few drops of vegetable oil to keep the spaghetti slippery.
4. Use different utensils to play with the spaghetti — tongs to pinch and pick up, chopsticks to wrap round, and roll up a fork to twizzle and twirl.

Taking it Higher:

Try mixing the colors together and creating a colorful palette of all the colors together. See what happens when you mix them up. How do the colors change? Take one strand of spaghetti out of the pot and measure it against another strand to see who has the longest strand of pasta. Use your own fingers for this pincer action and improve fine motor skills. Tasting is not recommended, but this activity is a fun touching experience and is very useful for practicing fine motor skills.

Added Value:

Play around further with the slimy spaghetti. Lay it out on the tray and move it around to make wavy lines of spirals. The tray may need some oil to allow the spaghetti to be moved into different shapes. Let older children write their names in slimy spaghetti noodles. Let the spaghetti dry on a board and voilà! — you have a name plaque for your child's room.

Fluffy to Frozen and Back Again

Here's an activity that incorporates the sense of touch in a variety of ways. Contrasts help children to learn about differences, and in the frozen or fluffy capacity, the pompoms provide exactly that kind of experience. The children can touch the fluffy pom-poms to see the before, and then the frozen pom-poms to discover the after-effects of the freezing process.

What You Need:
- Small fluffy pom-poms
- Different shaped containers (extra-large cookie cutters and bakers' moulds make wonderful shaped containers)
- Pipettes, forks, or other utensils
- Plastic tray or bowls

Steps:
1. Prepare the pom-poms by putting them into the shaped containers you have chosen. They could be cake moulds or special tins you have saved.
2. Add boiled cooled water. Boiled water freezes clearly, not in an opaque manner.
3. Freeze your heart containers.
4. Keep some of the pom-poms out of the containers to use for the experience of touching the dry fluffy pom-poms compared with the wet frozen ones.
5. When you are ready for your frozen activity, set the frozen heart on a tray with the different utensils needed to scrap, chip, and dig out the pom-poms.
6. Keep a bowl aside for the pom-poms as they are excavated.

Taking it Higher:

There are great language opportunities attached to this activity, like discussing the contrasts of the frozen or fluffy pom-pom, and the differences in temperature and texture. You also have the opportunity to try and connect the semi-frozen pom-poms together, as the ice may still be cold enough to touch the pom-poms together in a row. Holding a handful of pom-poms and squeezing tightly to see how much water comes out is another fun way to experience liquid and solid sensations.

Added Value:

Let the children return the pom-poms to the container when they have defrosted, ready for another frozen activity. Encourage them to make a pattern from the outside into the centre with the pompoms they have. When they are frozen for the second time, the shape can be turned out onto the tray and children could get colored stickers to copy the pattern they made with the pom-poms. Then, they will have a frozen pattern made out of colored stickers to represent their handiwork.

Sensory Hearts

This sensory heart activity brings the senses together through the tactile experience of colored rice grains and the designing of heart inserts in the colorful rice. Colored pom-poms add another dimension, as they are soft compared with the hard grains of rice. Tactile language like hard and soft, small and tiny, many and few, will also be practiced as this activity is enjoyed.

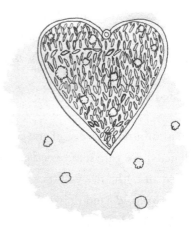

What You Need:
- Colored rice grains
- White rice grains
- Pom-poms in assorted colors
- A large tray
- Heart-shaped cookie cutters

Steps:
1. Color the rice grains using food coloring. Dry and set aside for the main color of rice to go on the tray.
2. Have white rice on hand for the fillers on the moulds or cookie cutters.
3. Prepare a tray to lay out the colored rice, ready to create the heart shapes.
4. Put the heart shapes into the rice on the tray but do not use colored rice inside the heart shape.
5. Pour white rice into the heart shape.
6. Use other heart shapes to fill with other colors or with the pom poms.
7. Remove the cookie cutters when they are filled and admire the beautiful heart shapes on the tray.

Taking it Higher:

Once the heart shapes have been removed, see if your child can match the correct shape to the cookie cutter that was used to make it. This is a good way to encourage perceptual skills, as well as to focus on texture and shapes.

Added Value:

Draw around the edge of the cookie cutter as if it were a stencil, then fill the stencil shape with some wood glue and sprinkle some of the colored rice over the glued area. The rice will stick to the glue. Underneath, write *"I have my heart stuck on you!"* and draw a little smile. This is a fun way to show appreciation for one another.

Slip and Slime on a Sandy Rainbow

Rainbows remind us of the magic of nature, and how after the rain comes the sun and a rainbow. Rainbow slime is the perfect sensory experience for little fingers and hands that like to experience their sense of touch through a medium that can slip through their fingers. The rainbow slime is slippery and slimy, and it holds its color and magical shimmer through the light — just like a real rainbow.

What You Need:
- Liquid starch
- Clear school glue
- Craft sand in assorted colors

Steps:
1. Mix equal quantities of starch and glue together.
2. Put different colors of sand in little piles in a bowl.
3. Mix and squeeze with your fingers. The mix is messy at first and will stick to itself. If it is too sticky, add more starch, and if it is too rubbery, add glue.
4. Mix the slime and the sand together and watch the rainbow colors appear.

Taking it Higher:

Messy mixing is the best sensory activity of all. Let your child say squishy squashy words as the slime is mixed together. Pull it and stretch it and look at it in the light. Have the slime run through their fingers, then pull it apart and mould it back together again. Describe how it feels and look at the colors. Do the colors change as the slime is mixed and played with?

Added Value:

Search and rescue games are always great fun. Pretend the slime is an alien trap sent to capture insects. Put plastic insects in the slime and have your child rescue the bugs, one by one. The game can be made more difficult, as the children could be blindfolded and required to find the bugs just using the sense of touch. Describing the insect and guessing what it is would be an added sensory experience.

Smell

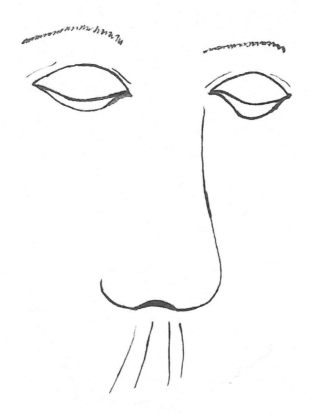

Smelling Station

Help the child develop a keen sense of smell with the creation of a smelling station. You can get family and friends involved in this activity, too, once the station is complete.

What You Need:
- Paper
- Pencil
- Rubber bands
- Small containers, such as jars
- Pieces of fabric cloths (one for each container)
- Variety of strong-smelling items

Steps:
1. Gather a few strong-smelling items and prep each one to add to a jar. For example, you can cut an orange or a lemon.
2. Have the child place a separate smelly item into a jar and cover the jar completely with a piece of fabric, ensuring the contents of the jar can't be seen.
3. Add a rubber band around the jar to keep the fabric secured.
4. Poke small holes through the fabric on the jar.
5. Have the child guess what he or she is smelling in each jar.
6. Take turns and have the child present the smelly jars to family members and friends and have them take a guess!

Added Value:

Talk about the most important sensory organ — the nose. Try smelling with a plugged nose. Try smelling with one nostril. Smell things that have an aroma through smoke, like incense or scented candles. Smell things where the aroma is carried on steam, like steaming bath salts or aromatic oils. Keep in mind that any activity involving heat should be closely supervised.

Taking it Higher:

Try making your own perfume. Collect rose petals or lavender flowers and leaves. Soak them, crush them, add an essential oil, and strain the liquid. Experiment with other leaves and flowers that have a scent, and use your sense of smell to decide how good your perfume is. Making scented creams can be a good sensory activity, too. Use a plain aqueous cream as the base and add essential oils to provide the aroma. What fun it would be to put little jars of cream together for gifts with pretty labels, to add a sense of joy in giving.

Fun Flowery Goo

Spring is a beautiful time of the year. This activity is a great way to appreciate spring flowers, and get a bit gooey at the same time. Collect some spring flowers or buds and make up some colorful oobleck. Then, see how your  senses engage as you feel the goo and coat the flowers in this strange, messy mixture.

What You Need:

- Cornflour and water mix for the oobleck
- Flowers, twigs, sturdy leaves, or buds
- Tray to hold the oobleck mixture
- Coloring for the oobleck mixture

Steps:

1. Mix up enough oobleck to half fill your tray. Add color of your choice.
2. Collect the plant material you plan to use for the experience.
3. Put the plant pieces on one side and experience oobleck with your hands, first. Then you are ready to slowly insert the plant material.
4. Watch what happens to each piece. Do some sink or float?

Taking it Higher:

Make the most of the oobleck and the different ways the garden items behave in the goo. Some may sink slowly, some may seem to float, and some will need some wiggling to get them fully coated with oobleck. These are all good talking points around the spring flower theme.

Added Value:

Look at the coated pieces and guess what they are. Ask your child to close his eyes or leave the room while you coat some garden bits and pieces in oobleck. Line them up on a tray and see if your child can tell you what each piece is. Or, try a squash-and-squeeze picture with a piece of folded paper. Put the colored piece of nature in between the sheets of paper and squash down. Then, open the paper and see what squashy picture you have made. Take a black marking pen and outline the shape to turn it into a squash monster. You can even add eyes and other features. There's lots of fun to be had as you appreciate the resulting squishy, squashy monster.

Cloud Nine Fluffy Flour Dough

Fluffy flour dough is a wonderful way to encourage sensory play. It is soft and malleable, and can be squashed, patted, squeezed, and moulded. Adding color, texture, and aroma to the dough increases its potential to delight the senses.

What You Need:
- Flour
- Oil (baby oil works well)
- Powdered or gel-based coloring, or non-toxic powder paint to color the dough
- Optional extras, like glitter or essential oils

Note: The proportions of oil and flour are on an 8:1 ratio — 8 cups of flour to 1 cup of oil, or 4 cups of flour to ½ cup of oil, or 2 cups of flour to ¼ cup of oil.

Steps:
1. Mix the oil and color together if using gel-based color, or, add the powder-based coloring or the non-toxic powder paint to the flour.
2. Combine the oil and the flour.
3. Blend it together to make a crumbly but kneadable mixture.
4. Add glitter for texture or essential oil for aroma.
5. Place different colors in separate containers, ready to be played with.

Taking it Higher:

This fluffy Cloud Nine dough offers wonderful sensory and fine motor opportunities — touch, smell, and maybe a lick of the lips, but not really a full-on taste experience. The dough is ideal for strengthening those small finger and thumb muscles. Kneading, pushing, pinching, and flattening the dough make good use of the muscles in your child's hand. The different sensations and the expression of ideas about the fluffy dough generate conversation as the dough is played with.

Added Value:

The sense of smell can be further enhanced by adding a unique scent to each different color. Play a game of "I can smell…" and use a blindfold over your child's eyes. Then, pass the various scented bowls of dough under their noses for a fun sensory guessing game. Add other smells into the game if you choose, like shampoo or moth balls or any household item with an identifiable smell. Guessing the smell will cause a lot of laughter and funny comments as you sniff the smelly dough and other aromas to see who can guess the smell under their noses.

Blindfold Sniff and Smell

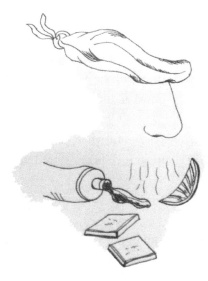

This is an entertaining game that makes good use of the sense of smell, and even makes a good party game. Primarily, it encourages participants to use their olfactory senses coupled with their knowledge of the items that might give off that particular aroma.

Since some children may be unfamiliar with the smells, let everyone smell the chosen scents prior to the game, and discuss what they are and where they are found. It may be possible to taste some of the items, and you can tell children how smell and taste go together as we won't eat things that don't smell good.

Try showing the children how the sense of smell is experienced through the nose. Talk about sniffing and smelling, and then try to smell while holding the nose and see if it works. Older children may also be interested in the anatomy of the nose.

What You Need:
- Small containers to hold the different objects to smell
- Five or six known ingredients to smell — for example lemon, cinnamon, chocolate, soap, and coffee, or toothpaste, shampoo, soap, hand cream
- A blindfold
- Paper to draw or write down guesses

Steps:
1. Collect the containers for the smell items.
2. Number them and fill them with the items to be sniffed.
3. Number the paper to correspond with the numbers on the containers.

4. Have your child leave the room while you set up.

5. Blindfold your child when you are ready to begin the mystery tasting game.

6. Depending on your child's writing ability, their answers to the numbered smelling pots can be recorded on the paper as a picture of the word, or have your child call out the answer and you can write it down according to the matching pots.

Warning: be careful when inhaling close to the pot, in case a powdery component may go up your child's nose and cause a lot of sneezing.

Taking it Higher:

This is a fun opportunity to discuss likes and dislikes, or good and bad smells. Order of preference would be a good activity, as it teaches the children to arrange items in order of preference. The idea of tasting each item after they have identified the smell would add another sensory dimension to the activity. Any item they do not want to taste may well be those they did not like the smell of.

Added Value:

Getting out magazines and looking for pictures of items that smell good is an added smell-related sensory activity. This could include non-edible items like flowers, perfumes, and soaps. You can also discuss the opposite of things that smell good and list some things that smell bad. Make a collage of items from a magazine that smell good and display the picture in a place where everyone can see and say, "Mmm, that smells so good!"

Smelly Soup!

Here's an opportunity to combine the sense of smell with some imaginative play and connections with nature. Making smelly soup starts with gathering the ingredients. Take a walk around the garden to pick anything with a perfume — roses are a good source of fragrance, as well as mint and other leaves and grass. Gather the smelly goodies in a tray with compartments or in a storage box.

What You Need:
- Collected leaves and grass and other items with a strong smell
- A tray or container to hold these items
- Items from the kitchen including vinegar for a bad smell and baking soda for an added fizzy sensation
- A bowl to mix the smelly soup in
- A wooden spoon

Steps:
1. Gather your smelly ingredients in the tray or container.
2. Have add-ins on standby, like vinegar and baking soda.
3. Put some water in the bowl you are planning to mix the smelly soup in and start to add different ingredients.
4. When you have reached the right smell, add the baking soda for the final fizz.

Added Value:

The sound of fizz at the end is an added sensory experience. Come up with some good stirring words and ways to develop vocabulary. Think of other mysterious noises that could be made to add value and fun to the sound effects.

Taking it Higher:

Combine imagination and the sense of smell to invent a spell that a witch might use to make the smelly soup. Describe each ingredient and what it smells like as they are added to the witches' brew. Add some food color to achieve a creepy effect, like red to look like blood. Dance around your brew and make up a song or cackle loudly to signify your pleasure and enjoyment of the smelly soup. Or, play a memory game like, "I went shopping and I bought…" and as each person 'buys' something, it is remembered and added to the list. In this instance, change the game slightly to say "I made smelly soup, and in it, I put…"

Tea Time With a Difference

Tea time is a chance to be sociable, relax, and take a break — and it's even more fun when you brew your own scented teas. Choosing a variety of items to try out different teas and then have a tea party is an exciting way to tap into sensory skills. Smell the tea as it brews and taste the result at your tea party.

What You Need:

- Coffee filter liners
- Variety of tea tastes to infuse — mint, rose petals, marshmallows, lemon peel, and any other ideas you may find in the panty
- Tea pot and cups for your guests
- Tags to label the different tea bags

Steps:

1. Take a coffee filter and fold it in half, then fold each side into the middle. Fold it in half again. Now you are ready to put the flavor into the funnel-shaped bag you have made. Fill the bag and fold down the top to staple it in place. Your specialty tea is now ready to dip into the boiled water and infuse before tasting.
2. Make little tags out of card, then punch a hole in the top to thread a piece of string through the tag and attach it to the ready-made bag.
3. Label the tag to suit the tea flavor.
4. An adult should boil the water and pour it into the teapot or per cup as the guests choose the flavor to taste.
5. Enjoy sipping tea and chatting together at your tea party.

Taking it Higher:

Create a little ritual of brewing the tea and then smelling the infusion before tasting. See if the senses of smell and taste go hand in hand, especially when new scents and flavors are experienced. Smelling the aroma of the tea is part of enjoying the taste.

Added Value:

Have a family tea-and-taste party, where everyone can sample each tea and choose their favorites. Include some tea biscuits to decorate to add different flavors and textures value to the party. It could be entertaining to have a Chinese tea ceremony, as well. This is an involved tradition, but talking about tea ceremonies may lead to an extension lesson on different cultures and how each enjoys the sense of peace attached to the tea ceremony. The cups and trays are set out beforehand, as well as the teapot and strainer, and the cups are warmed before the tea is poured. The sensory experience covers the warm feeling of the cups, the aroma of the tea, and the actual pouring ceremony. The cups are held in both hands and the tea is enjoyed through slow sips. Finally, the happy tea drinkers tap on the table to show their appreciation for the tea and the tea master.

Scented Dough

Making scented dough will send your child on a journey through their senses. This is an enjoyable tactile and olfactory activity. Smelling and touching are two important senses, and the act of kneading and breathing in the aroma of the scented dough provides opportunities to express feelings of joy, gladness, and appreciation.

What You Need:
- Flour
- Vegetable oil
- Optional extras — try lemon Kool-Aid with yellow chalk or pavement paint, or use other Kool-Aid flavors and other colors of chalk or pavement paint to create different flavors and colors

Steps:
1. Use 8 cups of flour to 1 cup of oil for a generous portion of dough. Scale down the amounts to 4 cups of flour to ½ cup of oil, or divide your flour and oil into different portions to experiment with other colors and flavors.
2. Knead together into a soft, mouldable consistency — not too wet and oily, and not too dry.
3. Crush the pavement chalk to add color and mix in the Kool-Aid in a related flavor for the scent.
4. Store in airtight containers or zip-lock bags.

Taking it Higher:

Scented dough is a sensory experience from start to finish. Measuring, mixing, and choosing the fragrance are all part of the initial tactile and language experience. Involve your child from the very beginning and talk through each process. There are also great opportunities for developing the small muscles in the hands through kneading, rolling, squashing, and squeezing actions. Roll the dough out with a rolling pin and use cookie cutters to make shapes. These actions are all ideal for building fine motor control. Pinching the dough is an excellent way to bring in the pencil-pinch exercise at the same time.

Added Value:

Creating dough in different flavors and colors lends itself to making a juicy bowl of fruit. If you have made different colors with different Kool Aid flavors, this could be a fun idea. Turn the colored dough into fruits and set them in a bowl. Once there are several fruits in the bowl, take turns wearing a blindfold and smelling and feeling the fruit shapes to play a "guess the fruit" game. After being blindfolded, one player picks out a piece of fruit from the bowl. First, they must describe it, and then they have a chance to smell the fruit and identify what fruit it is. This will require a variety of colors and flavors to make up a number of different fruits. This game gives children a good opportunity to make use of their senses of touch and smell together.

Sugar and Spice and All Things Nice Dough

Making a sensory play dough with all the spiced aromas of autumn is the perfect activity for a cool fall day. A basic cooked play dough recipe combined with seasonal coloring and added spices will fill your kitchen with a warm, autumnal smell. The play dough is soft to touch and moulds very well into the shape of any little critter that would be associated with this time of the year. Think about the actions of rolling up and curling into a ball, as some animals will be getting ready to hibernate.

What You Need:

- 1 cup flour
- 1 cup water
- 2 tsp cream of tartar
- ⅓ cup salt
- 1 tbsp oil
- A collection of spices to grind in a mortar and pestle

Steps:

1. Collect the spices you would like to grind in the mortar. Nutmeg, cinnamon, and cloves are a nice combination. Grind the spices with the pestle and set them on one side. Let your child join in the grinding process.
2. Prepare to make the dough. Put all the ingredients together in a pan and mix until there are no lumps BEFORE you put the mixture on the stove to heat up.
3. Your younger children can enjoy this process, too, because no heat is involved. Older children who may be ready to stir over the heat will still need supervision.

4. Stir over medium heat to cook the mixture. Let it thicken, then transfer to a tabletop.

5. Knead and roll out the dough. It is important to make sure it has cooled down before handling it.

6. Break the dough into manageable chunks for little fingers.

7. Finally, add the ground spices to the portions of dough and knead them in thoroughly. The smell of the spices and the dough will bring rich, sweet and spicy aromas to your child's attention.

8. Store the dough in a sealed container at room temperature for up to four months.

Taking it Higher:

The spiced dough offers added olfactory stimulation. Remind your child that he or she ground the spices from the beginning, and let them soak in the rich aroma of the fresh spices. Enjoy the wonderful sensation of pulling and rolling and squeezing the dough. Talk about how the smell of the spices gets stronger when the dough is warmed by rolling and squeezing. Use language skills to describe the actions and the senses used in this activity.

Added Value:

Discuss all the lovely spiced treats available this time of the year, like hot cross buns and donuts and other foods with cinnamon or nutmeg in them. Use the play dough to make buns or other tasty treats. Have a winter tea or chocolate treat event, and make sure each guest smells the cakes and exclaims about how wonderful they smell.

Tea for Two or Two for Tea

Flavored tea bags work wonderfully for an aroma matching game. Herbal and green teas provide a wide variety of different aromatic flavors. There are fruity flavors like lemon, berries, and peaches, along with spicy and herbal flavors like mint, vanilla, and chamomile. All these flavors are available in the tea section of your grocery store, and there are combinations of these flavors, too. Line up one set of tea bags, and then put the matching set into a basket or bowl. Each person takes a turn to choose a tea bag, then tries to match it to its twin on the table. Allow your child to smell the tea bags while they are still dry and in their sachets, and show your child how to squeeze the bag to encourage the aroma to be stronger.

What You Need:
- Flavored tea bags and their tags (have two of each flavor available for the matching process)
- Saucers or little pots to put the bags into for the additional "guess my smell" exercise

Steps:
1. Save the tea bags with the different aromas that you would like to use.
2. Remove the tags for matching purposes.
3. Number the bags and make a list of the flavors for yourself, so you know which tag goes with which bag.
4. Lay the bags out on their plate or container, ready for the smelling process.
5. Lay the tags out separately.
6. Let the children smell the bag and match it to a tag. Older children may be able to list the tags and match the bags.

Added Value:

The children may enjoy selecting their favorite aromas. When they have chosen a favorite, soak it in water and let the children taste the flavored tea. With older children, try laying the bags out in alphabetical order. Or, make a list of preferences from best smell to worst, and discuss why this is the chosen order. Feel the bags to include the sense of touch and increase the odour of the flavored tea bags.

Taking it Higher:

Try making your own flavored tea. Discuss with the children that the tea has to be made of dried ingredients, and then look for options. Look for spices like cinnamon or cloves and put them into pieces of muslin cloth tied at the top with a piece of string so the tea will infuse into the water. Try to dry some mint from the garden or herb shop, and when the mint is dry, add it into the muslin bag. Think of other dried items that could become a flavored tea product. There is lots of room for discussion here, and plenty of creativity — you can even design your own labels for your new variety of tea.

Taste

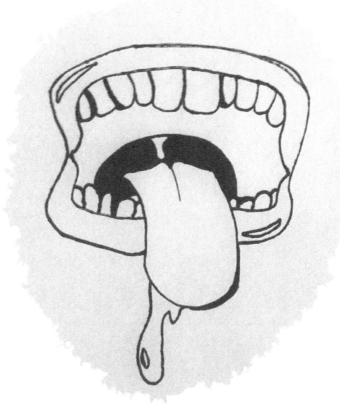

Slippery Jolly Jell-O Balls

Playing with Jell-O is one of the best slippery sensory activities — and it's totally edible. Jell-O balls are designed to entertain by slipping and sliding as they get squeezed and squashed. This activity requires some preparation the day before to set the Jell-O in the containers of your choice. Small ice cube trays to make round ice cubes are ideal for the small Jell-O ball molds, but larger kitchen bowls or chocolate moulds would be useful, too. Jell-O balls are a blast for children of any age, stimulating their taste buds and providing the sensation of slippery jelly in your child's mouth. This activity will always be a winner.

What You Need:
- Packets of Jell-O in different flavours and colors
- Bowl and water to mix — use slightly less water than the packet recommends to have a firmer setting to the Jell-O
- Shaped or round ice trays and containers to set the Jell-O in overnight

Steps:
1. Mix up your Jell-O and set in the fridge, ready for your activity.
2. Have a basin or activity tray to play with the Jell-O balls.
3. Mix colors together as the balls of Jell-O are squashed and handled.
4. Let the Jell-O be available in the large container to experience the sensations of Jell-O slipping through fingers.
5. Pat the Jell-O and feel how it wobbles.

Added Value:

The wobbly, sticky Jell-O adds a different sensation to the list of sensory perceptions — a wet, but not totally liquid sensation. It's gooey and oozey and can be held while these properties are explored. Mix various flavors of Jell-O and little fingers can enjoy a fun taste while they experience the texture of gooey jelly stuff. Another activity could involve guessing the flavors, like orange or lemon or strawberry, and so on, making for an engaging group activity.

Taking it Higher:

Here's a fun thing to try. Make the Jell-O in ice cube trays, then, when they are set, use the cubes to construct something. Create a pattern, a wall, a house — anything that could be built up and then squashed!

Super Gooey, Sludgie Slime

Sludgie slime is just the perfect tactile blob of goo that every child loves to handle. It's soft and smooth, squashy and squishy, and offers wonderful opportunities to experience the sense of touch. Sludgie slime is easy to make using basic kitchen ingredients. The materials are edible, too, so if a little piece happens to reach curious lips, sludgie slime will not upset delicate tummies. This slime is fun to play with on your own or in a group. Young and older children will love this goo!

Mix up the sludgie slime and let everyone enjoy the feeling of the goo as it slips through their fingers. It's easy to make and easy to store.

What You Need:
- 3 cups of corn starch (or corn flour)
- 1 cup of flour — adding flour makes the slime more doughy
- 1 ½ cups of cold water
- ¾ cup of chia seeds — they help absorb some of the water
- Food coloring to add to the water — just a drop or two, depending on how dark you want the color to be
- 2 packets of gelatin dissolved in 2 cups of hot water (adults will need to handle the hot water)
- Mixing bowl
- Wooden spoon
- Measuring cups
- Airtight storage container

Steps:

1. Pre-mix the gelatin with the hot water and store in the fridge overnight to let it set into a slimy mixture. This is something for an adult to do.
2. Combine all the dry ingredients in a bowl and mix together. Add the gelatin mix from the fridge and the colored water to your dry ingredients.
3. Mix the goo in the bowl and let it ooze through your fingers. Stretch it, squash it, and squeeze the slime until it becomes soft and gooey in your hands.
4. Older children can be part of the measuring and mixing, while younger children will enjoy pushing and pulling at the slime as it gets mixed together.

Added Value:

Tactile sensory play has enormous benefits for young children. The action of kneading the gooey slime strengthens the tiny muscles in the hands and wrist. Anxious children find the squashing and squeezing of the sludgie slime very soothing and helps to distract their minds from stressful situations.

Playing with the slime encourages social interaction and provides an opportunity to use vocabulary like squash and squeeze, or soft and smooth. Children will enjoy moulding the goo and then watching it spread as it oozes across the table or the floor. Try taking the gooey slime outside in a big basin and have fun squishing it through your toes.

Taking it Higher:

An entertaining idea older children may enjoy is making slugs from slime, then watching them slide down a kitchen tray or baking tray. Make your slugs and dampen the tray. Tip the tray at a slight angle and see how they slide.

Younger children may enjoy a story related to squashing and squeezing. Read Julia Donaldson's delightful story called *A Squash and a Squeeze*.

Super gooey sludgie slime goes a long way to educate and entertain!

Creative Rainbow Color Tasting

This activity ticks several sensory boxes. It's a tasty treat, a spectacular visual array of colors, and a chance to use fingers to touch and smooth the creamy, colorful mixture. The rainbow hues are made from whipped cream with color added — completely safe to lick, and delightful to feel with fingers.

What You Need:
- Whipped cream — not shaving cream
- Food coloring
- Snack trays or muffin pans
- Tray or paper
- Scooping spoons
- Extra bowls for white cream and mixing

Steps:
1. Prepare the mixing bowls and snack trays, ready to fill with the cream.
2. Whip the cream or buy ready-whipped cream to squirt into the trays.
3. Dip a toothpick or small lolly stick into the coloring to mix into each portion of whipped cream. You will only need a very small amount of color to tint the cream.
4. Mix the colors in the pans or tray, and leave an extra bowl of white cream for additional color mixing as needed.
5. Lay out a tray or white paper to spoon on the colors and make your rainbow.

Added Value:

The creamy paint is totally edible, so the artists can touch and taste as they mess around with the delightful colors. They can make rainbows or stripy patterns — whatever they find inspiring! This is a mix and mess activity, so be prepared for a bit of clean-up. Find a rainbow song to sing along with as you paint the rainbow colors.

Taking it Higher:

Change the tempo of the activity with ice cream. Using the same principles, but with vanilla ice cream, may be a great party trick — especially on a hot summer day. Make rainbow ice cream cones and finish them off with sprinkles and other edible decorations.

Summer Splash Watermelon Fun

There's nothing quite like the smell and taste of watermelon in the summer. Let your child watch as you cut open the giant melon and reveal its beautiful pink fruit, dotted with black pips. Touch, taste, smell and sight senses are all engaged here. Even sound is embraced as the melon is crushed and releases its juices.

Depending on your child's age, allow them to participate in cutting and tasting the fruit. Little ones will have to be supervised, or have their hands held to guide the cutting process. Another fun option is to use melon scoops to make flavorful watermelon balls to taste. Touching the melon and squishing it between their fingers as well as sipping up the sweet juice add exciting sensory experiences to this activity.

What You Need:
- Watermelon juice
- Kool-Aid watermelon flavors
- Cornstarch to make oobleck

Steps:
1. Slice the melon and scoop out the watermelon flesh.
2. Remove pips and extract the watermelon juice.
3. Add Kool Aid flavor to the juice for extra taste and smell effects (optional).
4. Use the cornstarch with the melon juice to create an oobleck consistency and experience a different sensation.

Taking it Higher:

The whole experience of using fresh watermelon to create a touch, taste, smell, and feel sensation is the benefit of this sensory lesson. Turn the exercise of cutting and squashing out the juice into a running commentary by describing each action as you work towards the final product of the watermelon oobleck. It is a sensory extension exercise, and offers a fantastic language opportunity, as well.

Added Value:

Never miss an opportunity to use some of the items from your lesson in a different way. The hollowed-out watermelon skin could make an interesting plant container. Let the children finish scooping out the inside, then flatten the bottom so the empty watermelon can stand on its own. Fill the outer part of the melon with soil and plant a few fast-growing seeds. Another fun idea is to make a face on the front of the melon, and then whatever grows will look like the hair of your creature. Merry melon monsters will look perfectly at home in the kitchen.

Little Picasso's Pudding Paint

Imagination and some colorful pudding paint are all you need for this tasty activity. Little artists will be excited to blend colors on a palette and spread edible paint all over their trays. Children will love feeling the soft, smooth texture of the pudding while enjoying a lick or two of delicious pudding paint as they create. And the best part is that if you don't like your masterpiece, just wipe away the errors, lick your fingers clean, and start again. This fun, flavorful activity will encourage conversation and sensory opportunities to touch and taste.

What You Need:
- Vanilla pudding made according to instructions on the packet
- Bowls and spoons
- Food coloring
- Baking trays or paper
- Wooden lolly sticks

Steps:
1. Mix the vanilla pudding and spoon it into different bowls, ready for adding color.
2. Mix more than one packet if there are several children or if you need more colors.
3. Mix the coloring with a lolly stick to create the "paint."
4. Have a tray or paper ready to paint on, even foil paper trays will do.
5. Get mixing and messing.

Added Value:

Using colored pudding paint is a finger-licking opportunity to explore color, texture, taste and pattern-making, all in one exercise. It is a simple, inexpensive activity. Your child will love finger painting with the different colors, or even using the lolly sticks like palette knives to scoop and scrape a picture or blend colors together. You can also suggest taking a piece of paper and folding it in half. Scoop blobs of pudding paint on one side, in no special pattern. Then, fold the unpainted half over the blobs and squash the paper down. When you open your paper back up, you'll see the butterfly or monster shape made by the squished paint.

Taking it Higher:

Make rainbow puddings by layering the colored pudding paint in a glass or transparent plastic container. Between each layer, add some chopped nuts, crushed cookies, or chocolate chips. Chill the rainbow puddings and eat them later as a special treat. Each layer will have a new crunchy, nutty, or chocolate taste and texture to enjoy and talk about as it is felt in each mouthful of pudding. Yum!

Berri Berri Nice Finger Paint

This is a wonderful way to create your own finger paints using only fruit. Blackberries are the best choice to crush and squeeze to extract vibrantly-colored juice. An added experience would be to collect the berries together, but if you  don't happen to have access to these delicious berries in your garden, the store-bought variety will be just fine. Show your child how to remove the stalks and squash out the juice. The fruit and juice can remain together in a dish, but if it's pure juice you're after, simply strain the fruit through a sieve and save the bright purple juice. Straining, squashing, and squishing out the juice are all wonderful sensory opportunities for little hands to enjoy. Feeling the soft fruit in between fingers and watching the juice run into the bowl is a perfect tactile experience, and a great chance to talk about the juice that comes from the fruit.

What You Need:
- Blackberries or other berries that are juicy and edible
- A bowl or jar to collect the juice
- A sieve, if required
- Old paint brushes
- Aprons or coveralls
- Water and soap to wash up afterwards

Steps:
1. Prepare the berries in a deep bowl.
2. Squash and squeeze the juice out of the berries.
3. Filter the fruit and juice through a sieve to separate the solid bits.
4. Set up a table covered with newspaper or a plastic cloth.

5. Cover the children participating with an apron or an old T-shirt — berry paint can stain clothing, so be careful.

6. Get into finger painting on the paper.

Added Value:

This is a chance to use fingerprints, thumb prints, and even handprints to explore and use the berry paint. The texture of the berry paint will be a fun sensory experience, as the berry pips and flesh are squeezed through the fingers and the juice drips into the bowl. Adventurous moms should be ready to let their finger painters experiment with their toes and feet, too — it's all part of healthy sensory development.

Taking it Higher:

Try painting with textures. Sponges dipped in the berry paint and dabbed onto paper give a totally different look. You could even cut out shapes from an old bathroom sponge and use them as stamps. Or, try painting with cotton buds or cut and stamp with potato slices to create designs using the bold berry dye. Fingerprints can be turned into patterns, or you could experiment by making thumbprint animals. There are tons of ways to explore the senses using Berri Berri Nice Finger Paint.

Hit and Miss on a Watermelon

There is so much fun to be had with this sensory activity. Your child can feel the watermelon and then enjoy hammering in the golf tees to completely change the texture of the melon. Then, there is the distinctive sound of the tapping as the tees are driven into the skin of the fruit. And, added to the sensory experience, your child will be developing both fine and gross motor skills by using the hammer to hit the tee, and practicing small fine motor actions to set the tee up for the activity.

What You Need:
- Watermelon cut in half
- Golf tees
- Wooden or rubber mallet

Steps:
1. Cut the watermelon in half lengthwise to create a steady surface to work with.
2. Scoop out the contents for a delicious fruit salad later.
3. Get the tees ready and show your child how to hold a tee carefully while hammering it into the watermelon. It may be advisable with younger children to get the tee set up and ready to hammer without using little fingers to hold it in place. Children will love the whole experience of tapping or hammering the tees into the melon.

Taking it Higher:

Talk about the sweet smell of the melon as the tees penetrate the skin and the juice comes out. Taste some of the contents of the melon and feel the black shiny pips. All these actions use the senses to enjoy the experience. Feel the skin before the tees are hammered in and then touch it again afterwards. If the tees went right through, feel around on the inside of the melon, as the tip of the tees will make the skin feel spiky.

Added Value:

This activity has great potential to add pattern-making and letters into the mix. Let your child design patterns using different colored tees. Or, use a black marker to draw on the skin of the melon, creating dots to mark specific points for the tees to be hammered in – maybe the tees can be hammered in to spell out a name. Get really creative and turn your melon into a spiky hedgehog. After the tees have been hammered in, a pair of eyes drawn on the front and another golf tee for a nose will create the illusion of a funky hedgehog.

Instant Ice Cream

If you are looking for a great way to entertain and have a bit of super cool fun, then making your own ice cream is just the right activity. It's so exciting to bag up the cream, surround it with ice, then shake a bit and — voilà! — you've made your own ice cream. Your child will go wild with excitement, as the results are almost instant and, of course, everyone loves ice cream.

Making ice cream also encourages the experience of touch sensations, thanks to the cold ice cream and the ice cubes used to start the freezing process. Be sure to encourage comments about how it feels and how the ice cream tastes, as this is a great opportunity to sample the cream as a liquid before the activity and then taste the frozen ice cream afterward. Touch and taste sensations go hand in hand to make this a wonderful sensory experience.

What You Need:
- ½ cup cream or milk (cream works best, or you can try almond milk to avoid lactose)
- 2 sandwich bags
- Chocolate syrup or vanilla (add a bit of sugar if you decide to make vanilla)
- A one-gallon bag and a grocery bag
- ¼ cup salt (table or rock)
- Sprinkles and decorations, if you want to have a party!

Steps:
1. Measure out the milk or cream.

2. Pour it into the first sandwich bag and add the flavor — either chocolate syrup or vanilla with a little sugar to taste.

3. Seal the first sandwich bag and place into another sandwich bag, then seal.

4. Place the two sealed bags into a one-gallon bag. Fill the bag with lots and lots of ice.

5. Add the salt to the ice and seal the gallon bag, too.

6. Finally, place the gallon bag into a grocery bag.

7. Now it's time to shake things up and get the ice moving — do this for eight minutes.

8. The ice cream should be ready, so carefully open the bags and very carefully remove the ice cream from the first sealed bag.

9. Eat the ice cream quickly before it melts — and remember to add decorations if you want to jazz up the whole delicious experience.

10. Enjoy!

Taking it Higher:

There are so many opportunities during this activity for sensory development, as well as for having fun and socializing. The experience of watching the ice and salt transform the milk or cream into ice cream is sure to generate amazement and delight. Seeing the liquid freeze into a solid and feeling the cold ice in the process will encourage language development and expressive comparisons of the textures and tastes. Introduce some movement or actions to make shaking the ice to create the ice cream even more fun and interactive.

Added Value:

The whole idea of making ice cream lends itself to having a little party time, too. Add in some sprinkles, chocolate chips, wafers, and any other ice cream extras you can think of. Decorate the ice cream and then, it's party time. Turn on the music and dance. It's always great to share the making and the enjoying of the dish together.

Ooey Gooey Chia Seed Slime

Every kid loves a bit of slime, and moms enjoy a mess-free activity — and the ooey gooey slime made with chia seeds is no exception. This is a no-cook recipe and the slime, with a sprinkling of textured chia seeds, will give endless fun. It is super stretchy and super gooey, and moves in one big blob. And, as an added bonus, the slime is edible! While this is not to be encouraged, if a bit slips into a toddler's mouth it is not harmful.

What You Need:
- ¼ cup chia seeds
- 2 cups water
- Plastic sealable container
- 1 tsp xanthan gum
- Food color
- Full box of cornstarch (corn flour)

Steps:
1. Soak the chia seeds in a plastic container overnight.
2. Stir once to avoid lumps.
3. The following day, stir again and add 1 tsp of Xanthan gum, then whisk.
4. Add three or four drops of food color, if you like.
5. Add a full box of cornstarch (corn flour). Mix and knead by hand.
6. Watch the consistency and add more corn flour if the substance is too sticky.
7. If the substance is too crumbly or dry, add a teaspoon of water at a time until you reach the desired consistency.
8. Store in the fridge in a sealed container. Remould the slime for future uses by wetting your hands to increase the elasticity.
9. Flax seed is an alternative to chia seeds — use ½ cup of flaxseed and 2 cups of water. Store in the fridge and add 2tsp xanthan gum. If you don't have access to chia seeds, the flax seeds work well, instead, but

you will need about ¼ of a cup more corn starch to mix into the flax seed mixture.

10. If you don't have access to any seeds, it is possible to make the slime without them. n this case, add 1 3/4 cups water to 1 tbsp xanthan gum. Whisk and add food color, if desired. Add one box of starch and ½ cup extra and mix together. Again, add more starch if it is sticky or more water if it is crumbly.

Taking it Higher:

Now you have the best slime ever! It is stretchy and slimy, and you can pull it out and squash it down. This slime will return to a blob as it is dropped on the table. Pull it apart and push it together. Let the slime ooze through little fingers and use creative language to describe how it feels. Hold the slime up to the light and enjoy the way the colors change.

Added Value:

This slime is so adaptable — it makes great handprints and even footprints. Spread out the slime and press hands into the goo. Wipe some watercolor paint over the print and press a piece of paper onto the print. Then have a look at the print on your paper. After, try the same thing with a footprint. Have further fun with cut out letters and shapes, or just enjoy the feeling of scooping up the blob and returning it to a ball of slippery slime.

Fruit Salad with a Difference

This is a juicy experience with fruit. Cut fruit served in a big bowl of water makes for an interesting hands-on touch and taste activity. The sensory awareness created through sight, smell, touch, and taste are all part of this delicious fruit salad sensation. This activity  keeps children busy for ages as they capture all the floating fruit pieces.

What You Need:
- A large bowl or plastic bath filled with water
- Different types of fruit suitable for cutting and floating in the water
- Knife and chopping board (for adult use only)
- Utensils to play with while capturing the fruit — like tongs, spoons, scoops, or strainers
- Food coloring an optional extra

Steps:
1. Prepare the fruit by cutting it in different ways. An orange, for example, can be sliced in half through the middle or cut into segments. Apples cut to show pips give an added dimension. Just make sure you stick to fruits that won't disintegrate in the water when handled.
2. Set up the large container with water and add the fruit. The more the merrier for this activity — if there are several children, a bigger bath and more fruit leads to even greater fun.
3. Let the children scoop up fruit and inspect each piece they collect before returning it to the water. Let them play with different utensils and see how the water runs through the strainer but the fruit does not.
4. When the interest is dying down a bit, add some food coloring to the water and see how the various fruits absorb the color.

Taking it Higher:

This is an opportunity to learn about different kinds of fruit. See if your child can fish with the strainer for some oranges or apple slices and so on, depending on the varieties you have chosen. Try some fruit tasting and group the fruits according to sweet or sour fruit. Look at colors and shapes and sort the fruit by putting them in dishes to inspect their unique qualities.

Added Value:

While you have pieces of cut fruit and a messy area going on, this would be a good opportunity to extend the concept through some fruit printing and pattern-making. Set out some paint colors — two colors will do the trick — on a plate. Dip the cut fruit in the paint and press them onto paper to make fruit patterns. The fruit is really wet, so thick paint will work well. Make patterns of fruit shapes in various colors.

Sound

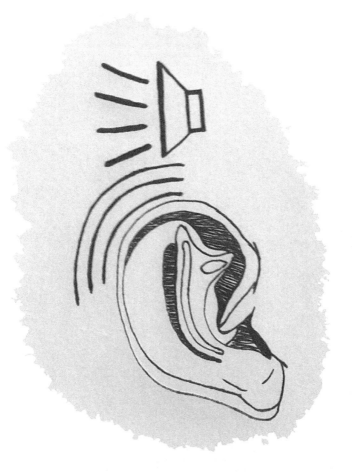

Plastic Bag: Low-Flying Kite

Here's an activity that everyone can enjoy and is sure to use up a great deal of energy. Flying kites is an age-old form of entertainment and this kite, made from a recycled plastic bag, is no exception. The cost of making the kite is virtually nothing and it is ready in minutes. The art of flying this kite is also incredibly simple. Once the kite is made, it acts like a windsock — all you do is pull it behind you, running into the wind.

It's exciting to feel the tugging of the string as the kite pulls in the breeze, and to hear the rustling noise of the plastic. The experience allows kids to listen to a variety of new sounds, explore the feel of plastic as it is flattened, and then watch as the kite fills with wind and flies behind them as they run. This activity is fun for all ages, but especially for younger children who might need to burn off some of their boundless energy.

So.... get ready to go fly a kite!

What You Need:
- Fairly large plastic shopping bag
- String or strong wool

Steps:
- Simply take the plastic bag and tie some string or wool to each of the handles. Join those two strings to another towing string, to make the kite easier to handle.
- Keep the string just long enough so it can fly away from your little kite runner!

Added Value:

Flying a kite is a great way to release tension and is a perfect chance to enjoy running around. The low-flying kite gives just the right amount of entertainment without all the complications of trying to get the kite up into the sky. Reserved children will just love this distraction, as the kite will be their focus — not any insecurities they may have. It is a sociable activity as children can fly their kites together, but does not require too much interaction for the reserved child.

Taking it Higher:

Older children will benefit from knowing about recycling and how we need to reuse plastic items whenever we can. They will grasp the reason why running into the wind will cause the kite to fill with moving air and 'fly.'

The kites can be decorated a variety of ways. On the back, try tying on something light like paper streamers to make them fly out in the wind. You can also draw fun faces or patterns on the plastic with permanent marking pens, which will add some personality to the low-flying kites.

Running kite races in the park or playground adds some competition and camaraderie to the kite flying.

Beep Beep the Hungry Robot

Feeding the tin bucket robot after artfully creating his funny face makes for a great game for all ages — it combines the senses of sight and sound and encourages kids to practice pattern-making and ordering of objects.

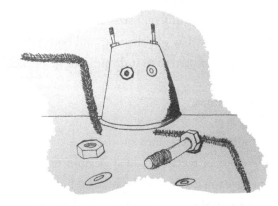

The fantastic sounds of metal clinking and clanking as "foods" are fed to this greedy robot are great for helping little ears focus on the sense of sound. This is a wonderful opportunity to use fine motor skills, too, as the nuts and bolts are threaded onto pipe cleaners.

What You Need:
- A small metal bucket
- A selection of nuts, bolts, and washers — anything of this genre that can be threaded or tossed in the bucket to feed the robot
- Pipe cleaners
- Stick-on alphabet letters to create the robot's face — if you are feeling creative, try cutting out funny parts of faces from magazines to put together a robot face

Steps:
1. Decorate your bucket to look like a robot.
2. Collect the nuts, bolts, and other metal goodies to feed your robot.
3. Make patterns of the nuts and bolts as they are threaded on the pipe cleaners, ready to be fed to the robot.
4. When the pattern is ready, drop the metal into the bucket one by one and listen to the wonderful clanking and clattering sounds they make.
5. Try a variety of sizes of metal to experience different sounds.

Taking it Higher:

Encourage pattern-making linked to sound as your child associates the various sounds with the different sizes and weights of the metal objects thrown into the hungry robot. Lay out the nuts and bolts and washers to make a pattern, then listen to your pattern as it drops into the bucket.

Added Value:

Try some magnetic tape on the back of some of the bigger nuts and washers. These bits of metal should stick onto the sides of the bucket. Now your child can have fun decorating the metal robot from the outside with a pattern around the base or the top of the bucket. The magnet sticking on the side is good fine motor control, too, as the magnetic piece has to be pulled off carefully from the side of the bucket.

Song of the Seeds

This activity is all about listening to the sounds of different seeds. Gather a broad selection of seeds in various sizes, from big haricot beans down to tiny lentils or miniature carrot seeds, and store each type in a small jar. Then, cover the jar in aluminum foil so the seeds are not visible. The children are tasked with identifying the seeds only by the sound they make when they are being shaken. This is a real test of listening skills, as there are no other senses to rely on.

What You Need:
- A variety of seeds, beans, popcorn, peas, lentils, etc.
- Small jars with a lid — bead jars are ideal for this
- Aluminum foil
- Pencil and paper

Steps:
1. Select as many different seeds as possible from your kitchen or from the supermarket.
2. Divide the seeds amongst the little jars so that they can be shaken.
3. Cover the jars with foil to ensure the seeds are not visible.
4. Get ready to listen to the 'song of seeds.'

Added Value:

This is a great opportunity to rely on the sense of sound as each jar is shaken and the noises made by the different seeds listened to carefully. Do they sound heavy or light? Do they sound like popcorn seeds ready to pop, or do they sound like tiny little seeds to grow some small vegetable? Could they be husky sunflower seeds for a parrot? The sound of the seeds could also lead to discussions about what the various seeds are used for.

Taking it Higher:

Ordering or grading objects is an important life skill. Use the seeds to listen to their sound and then put them in a size order according to the sound they make. When you have decided on their order, peel back the foil and see if your assessment was right. Any wrong sizes can be discussed to identify why they were put in the wrong order, and everyone can listen again to hear the size of the seed correctly. Make up a little rhythm shake-shake song using the different seed jars. Or try shaking out well-known nursery rhymes and see if the other members of the family can guess the tune. Organize yourselves into a group and get ready to shake up a seedy song.

Shake Rattle and Roll

This activity creates a sensory sound experience using seeds and other objects to shake, rattle, and roll! Using different seed sounds, it is possible to have a celebration of natural music. The sound theme encourages experiments with seeds and the variety of noises they make when they are rattled.

In this experiment, children can shake up different objects that will fit into the small jars you have decided to use. Collect various items that will shake and rattle, like seeds or marbles and so on. Store them in covered containers and get ready to shake up a lot of seedy sounds as you try to guess the origins of each noise.

What You Need:
- All kinds of seeds, coins, marbles, bells, Lego bricks, water, rice, and so on — anything that will go into a small jar and can be shaken
- Small jars with lids
- Something to cover the jars so the contents cannot be seen like tin foil, tape, or dark paper

Steps:
1. Find several small jars with lids to fill with the seeds or other items you plan to shake.
2. Make two of each kind to be ready for a different game.
3. Put a few of each kind of seed in each jar.
4. Seal the lid and cover the jars so the contents cannot be seen.
5. Aluminum foil is a good covering, because it can mould around the jar.

6. Number the jars to help with identification, but keep the list to yourself.
7. Shake the contents and guess what is inside each jar.
8. Take out the matching jars one at a time and see if your child can rattle the jars and find the jar with the matching sound.

Added Value:

This is an opportunity to focus on the sense of hearing, because the other senses are blocked during this experience. You cannot see, taste, or touch the items in the jar — you rely purely on the sense of sound. What noise do you hear as you rattle the jar? Do some sounds seem heavier or lighter as the jar is rattled? Heavier items sound like bass sounds, and lighter objects are closer to soprano sounds. Discuss musical differences. Can you match the sounds of the jars that make the same noise?

Taking it Higher:

Start a band session! Use the jars like shakers and add in some pots to bash for drums and any other objects you can come up with that could make sounds. Put all the sounds together in the form of a band and try to bash out a simple nursery rhyme, like "Three Blind Mice." You could also try echoes, where one person puts together a series of sounds and the other person copies them like an echo.

Big Band Sounds

Making music by playing with elastic bands and strumming is similar to many string instruments. How does the sound of the elastic band reach our ears? This experiment is an interactive way to show children how sound reflects off other objects. When sound can reflect or echo from another surface, we hear it loud and clear. When sound is dulled or muffled by something that absorbs it, like cloth, we do not hear it as well. Children can come to understand about acoustic sound through this simple but fun demonstration of sound.

What You Need:
- Elastic bands — try to use bands of different thicknesses if possible, but this is not essential
- A plastic cup
- A cloth — maybe a dishcloth or small towel

Steps:
1. Start off by strumming a band between your two fingers. Stretch an elastic band between your thumb and forefinger and then, while it is taut, pluck at the elastic. What do you hear?
2. Wind different widths of elastic bands over the top of a cup. Now pluck or strum these bands. Listen to the different sounds made with the different rubber bands.
3. Using the same cup and the bands stretched over the top, push a tea towel or cloth into the cup, ensuring that while the cup is full of cloth, the bands are still free to be played. Pluck the bands and listen to the difference in the sound.
4. Ask why the sound is different — because the cloth has absorbed the sound instead of reflecting it, as was the case when the cup was empty.

Added Value:

Experiment with other bands and various ways of strumming or plucking them. Each time you change the pattern of what you do, there will be a different result, a different sound. Take the experiment further by pulling the bands over other containers and listening to the different sounds you can make. Look at some musical instruments and discuss the sound from the big bass instruments, as well as the smaller string ones. Talk about sound and music and how various instruments create their sound. Banging, plucking, strumming, and so on are all ways of creating sound effects. Use the sense of sound to discover sound levels like loud and soft, and different pitch levels like high and low.

Taking it Higher:

Have fun making a musical instrument. See if you can find different sizes of boxes and create a variety of sounds. If there are enough 'musicians' around, you can even create a band. Playing together and adding drums and shakers would create a wide range of sounds. Encourage your child to talk about the noises being made by the different instruments. Playing some band music and asking the children to raise their hand when they hear the drums, cymbals, or other instruments will encourage listening skills and learning to pick out a particular noise out of a collection of sounds.

Hanging on Musical Notes

Imagine being able to experience the basic principle of sound waves right in your own home. Using a simple wire coat hanger and some string, you can show your child how to feel and hear sound waves! It's an abstract concept, but looking at leaves or a flag blowing in the wind may help with the concept of sound travelling without being seen, just like the wind. Listening while feeling the vibrations of the string will add a more tangible realness to this abstract idea. Sound is not something we can see, but we can feel vibrations and hear music, as sound is carried to our ears through vibration.

What You Need:
- A wire coat hanger
- Some string

Steps:
1. Tie a piece of string around the middle of a wire coat hanger.
2. Wrap the string around your index finger and hold the strings next to your ears.
3. Bang the hanger onto the edge of a table or another object.
4. Feel the vibrations from the wire hanger and sense the sound waves coming towards you. Try lengthening or shortening the string for different effects.

Added Value:

Look and feel other vibrations through things like whistles, vibrating speakers, wind blowing, and humming. Talk about noise and nature, and the different sounds are all around us. Think about big bands and all the various ways they make music.

Taking it Higher:

It is possible to see vibrations by setting a vibrating object in water and watching the ripples as the sound waves disturb the water. A tuning fork is the ideal vibrating instrument to visualize sound waves, but not everyone has access to such a device — but any metal object that vibrates when it is plucked or pulled will do the trick.

Rhythm of Rain

Listening to the sound of falling rain is very relaxing — and knowing you can capture that sound in a jar is even more exciting! Make rain shakers together and then ask your child to close their eyes and listen to the soothing sound of rain as the shaker is turned and the contents create that familiar noise. Spend some time describing the sound of the gently falling rain.

What You Need:
- A bottle with a lid
- Dry sticks or twigs
- Rice

Steps:
1. Take a nature walk in the garden and collect some dry twigs that will fit into the bottle you have chosen.
2. Pour in around a handful of rice.
3. Seal the jar, and you have a musical rain shaker.
4. You can shake the jar for a rush of rain or you can simply turn the bottle over and listen to the gentle sound of the rice grains running through the sticks, sounding just like rain.

Added Value:

This activity offers wonderful opportunities to discuss rain and the effects of rain — or, the opposite effect having no rain. Listen to the sounds and talk about what you do on rainy days. Discuss how it smells when it rains on the ground after a long period of dry weather. And how about the sound of rain on the roof, and the sensation of rain falling on your skin? What do you wear when it rains? There are endless ways to talk about rain — all with the senses of sight, sound, and touch attached to the vocabulary and discussion.

Taking it Higher:

Have fun making up your own rain dance and using your rain shakers to create the sound of the rain and that natural music. If you have some feathers around, you can make a headdress of feathers to wear for your rain dance. The feathers represented the wind, and wearing something turquoise represented the water or rain. This rain dance will be a creative expression of the inspiring sound of the rain. And who knows — perhaps it may even rain after your dance!

One, Two, Three - Listen to Me

Helping children learn listening skills is a vital part of school readiness. In fact, throughout a child's school career, listening is a very important part of learning. These three activities encourage the sense of hearing and foster better listening skills.

Each activity covers a different sound technique. The first, like the notes on a xylophone, helps children listen to sound in increasing or decreasing tones. The children tap the glasses and can work out that the different volumes of water affect the tone of the sound. The second activity makes use of various dried contents in plastic eggshells. The listening skill is to associate larger items with a heavier tone of sound. Finally, the third sound game is one that uses items around the house and their common noises. With eyes closed, the children can only hear the sound as they try to relate it to the everyday noises they hear all the time.

Each activity is simple, fun, and easy to do at home. A child's sense of hearing can become dulled by listening to the same things all the time, so this activity will help stimulate that sense while all the objects are right there in your child's home.

What You Need:
- Glasses of jars to put water into
- Something to tap the jars
- Plastic egg containers, like the ones used at Easter. They open and can be filled with different small objects like beads, seeds, clips, etc.
- Something to seal the eggs once they are filled, like duct tape or masking tape
- A list of different sounds around the house, like a doorbell, drawers opening, or a gate closing

Steps:

1. Set up your jars of water to make a water xylophone. Each jar should have a different amount of water in, so it will make a different sound.

2. Play with your water xylophone by tapping the various jars. Arrange them in size order and hear how the sound changes with the level of water.

3. Collect a number of the plastic eggs.

4. Open the plastic eggs and fill them with different small items that will make a rattling sound. Make matching pairs of eggs and see if the children can work out which two sound the same. Seal the eggs carefully prior to starting to ensure they don't burst open.

5. Make a list of items around the house that make a noise, like a doorbell, a drawer opening, or a teaspoon in a cup. Make sure your child cannot see what you are doing as you make these sounds — it's their job to guess what objects are creating the noises.

Added Value:

These three activities are all about encouraging the sense of hearing. Make sure you stress the action of listening and hearing using the sense of sound. Highlighting the common sounds around the house build awareness of what is frequently heard at home. Take the activity higher by practicing with sounds heard in the city. Develop various themes of sound, and discuss sounds of the farm, sea sounds, and other sounds from other settings or events. Add vocabulary development by talking about how certain sounds make you feel.

Taking it Higher:

Enjoying the sense of sound is part of the experiment with the water xylophone. Tell the children about the musical notes on a piano, and how they go up and down according to the pitch of the sound, based on the amount of water in the container. When the notes go up or down in range on the piano, these are musical scales. If you are lucky enough to have a piano close by, you can demonstrate these scales for the child. Now arrange your water bottles from smallest to largest and tap them accordingly — your child is playing musical scales. Try an easy tune, like a nursery rhyme. All this musical sound experience is encouraging both listening and hearing.

Acknowledgements

Thank you to all the people who contributed to the making of this book, including those who provided a writing space, parents and educators who volunteered to review this book, our editors, and illustrator.

About the Author

Mary McPhee has been a special educator for more than 40 years, helping young children and teens with autism and sensory processing disorder learn and thrive.

With advanced education and training in sensory integration, she has worked with children both in their homes and in local schools. She has also worked collaboratively with early childhood educators, speech pathologists, physical therapists, psychologists, and physicians.

She is commissioned regularly by school systems and associations to give seminars for early education teachers and other professionals on sensory, motor, and social skills.

Mary is a big advocate of learning through play, and she regularly contributes to parenting for special needs magazines. Her writing has enlightened and inspired parents, educators, and caregivers around the world.

Mary currently lives and works in Montreal, Canada.

About the Illustrator

Seth Priske from Oshawa, Ontario, was diagnosed with high functioning ASD and ADHD as a child. He discovered his love for art at an early age, drawing anything and everything — particularly images related to his fixation of dinosaurs.

With continuous growth along the way, his creative flame became stronger when music was found to be another strong interest and reinforced the two energy-driven tasks as one, the creative drawing has blossomed into a range of full-page, felt-tip, brightly-colored journeys. Sharing his gift of artistic talent has been his main focus, first and foremost.

More Autism Handbooks

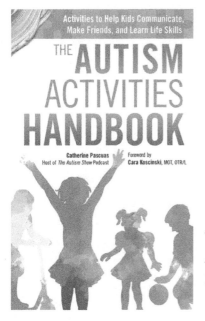

The Autism Activities Handbook:
Activities to Help Kids Communicate,
Make Friends, and Learn Life Skills

Social Skills Handbook for Autism:
Activities to Help Kids Learn Social Skills
and Make Friends

Both books are available in ebook and
print formats.
www.AutismHandbooks.com

The Autism Show Podcast

Visit *The Autism Show* website, www.AutismShow.org, for free interviews with autism experts and resources on autism.

You'll find free interviews with the best minds in the field and hear from parents and adults on the autism spectrum. *The Autism Show* podcast focuses on positivity, and on the progress that individuals on the autism spectrum can achieve.

We are proud to provide resources to help people on the autism spectrum and their families achieve independence, productivity, and happiness.

www.AutismShow.org

Made in United States
Orlando, FL
16 November 2023

39067630R00085